Reading Drills

Jamestown's Reading Improvement

Edward B. Fry Ph.D.

JAMESTOWN  PUBLISHERS

a division of NTC/CONTEMPORARY PUBLISHING GROUP
Lincolnwood, Illinois USA

Cover Design: Lightbourne

ISBN: 0-8092-0361-8
Published by Jamestown Publishers,
a division of NTC/Contemporary Publishing Group, Inc.,
4255 West Touhy Avenue,
Lincolnwood (Chicago), Illinois 60712-1975, U.S.A.
© 2000 NTC/Contemporary Publishing Group, Inc.

Manufactured in the United States of America.

11 12 13 14 ROV 15 14 13 12 11 10

Acknowledgments

Acknowledgment is gratefully made to the following publishers, authors, and agents for permission to reprint these works. Every effort has been made to determine copyright owners. In the case of any omissions, the Publisher will be pleased to make suitable acknowledgments in future editions.

"Magic Spinach: A Chinese Folk Tale" translated by Carol Eron and Fulang Lo. *Cricket*, June, 1994, Vol. 21.

"How to Lasso a Shark" by William B. McMorris. Reprinted by permission of *Boys' Life* Magazine. Published by the Boy Scouts of America.

"Tuck Everlasting" excerpt from *Tuck Everlasting* by Natalie Babbitt. Copyright © 1975 by Natalie Babbitt. Reprinted by permission of Farrar, Straus & Giroux, Inc.

"Mystery Monsters of Loch Ness" from *Mystery Monsters of Loch Ness* by Patricia Lauber. © 1978 by Patricia Lauber. Used by permission of the author.

"The Great Brain at the Academy" from *The Great Brain at the Academy* by John D. Fitzgerald. Copyright © 1972 by John D. Fitzgerald. Published by Bantam Doubleday Dell Books for Young Readers by arrangement with Dial Books for Young Readers, a division of Penguin Books, USA, Inc.

"From the Mixed-Up Files of Mrs. Basil E. Frankweiler" reprinted with the permission of Atheneum Books for Young Readers, an imprint of Simon & Schuster Children's Publishing Division from *From the Mixed-Up Files of Mrs. Basil E. Frankweiler* by E. L. Konigsburg. Copyright © 1967 E. L. Konigsburg.

"Mom, You're Fired!" from *Mom, You're Fired!* by Nancy K. Robinson. Copyright © 1981 by Nancy K. Robinson. Reprinted by permission of Scholastic, Inc.

"We Live in Mexico" from *We Live in Mexico* by Carlos Somonte. Copyright by Carlos Somonte. Reprinted by permission of the publisher, Franklin Watts, Inc.

"James and the Giant Peach" from *James and the Giant Peach* by Roald Dahl. Copyright © 1961 by Roald Dahl. Copyright renewed 1989 by Roald Dahl. Reprinted by permission of Alfred A. Knopf, Inc.

"Little House in the Big Woods" from *Little House in the Big Woods* by Laura Ingalls Wilder. Text copyright 1932 by Laura Ingalls Wilder; copyright renewed 1959 by Roger Lea MacBride. Used by permission of Harper Collins Publishers, Inc. "Little House" ® is a registered trademark of Harper Collins Publishers, Inc.

"Racing on the Wind" from *Racing on the Wind* by E. and R. S. Radlauer. Copyright © 1974 by Edward and Ruth S. Radlauer. Reprinted by permission of Franklin Watts, Inc.

"Henry Reed's Journey" from *Henry Reed's Journey* by Keith Robertson. Copyright © 1963, renewed © 1991 by Keith Robertson. Used by permission of Viking Penguin, a division of Penguin Putnam, Inc.

"The Good-Guy Cake" from *The Good-Guy Cake* by Barbara Dillon. Copyright © 1980 by Barbara Dillon. Published by Morrow Junior Books (a division of William Morrow and Company, Inc.).

"The Enormous Egg" from *The Enormous Egg* by Oliver Butterworth. Copyright © 1956 by Oliver Butterworth; copyright © renewed 1984 by Oliver Butterworth. By permission of Little, Brown and Company (Inc.).

"Paul Bunyan Swings His Axe" from *Paul Bunyan Swings His Axe* by Dell J. McCormick. Reprinted by permission of Caxton Press of Caldwell, Idaho.

"Birth of an Island" from *Birth of an Island* by Millicent E. Selsam. Text copyright © 1959 by Millicent E. Selsam. Published by Harper & Row Publishers, Inc.

"Hotel for Dogs" from *Hotel for Dogs* by Lois Duncan. Copyright © 1971 by Lois Duncan. Reprinted by permission of Harold Ober Associates Incorporated.

"Set Your Sails for Fun!" by Jennifer Albert, published in *Youth 87*, November–December, Vol. VII, No. 7, p. 26.

Contents

	To the Student	1
Sample	Dowsing: Fact or Fiction	4
1	Magic Spinach *translated by Carol Eron and Fulang Lo*	8
2	The Year Without a Summer *by Henry and Melissa Billings*	12
3	The Three Brothers and the Treasure *by José Maria and Eça de Queiroz*	16
4	How to Lasso a Shark *by William B. McMorris*	20
5	Tuck Everlasting *by Natalie Babbit*	24
6	Mystery Monsters of Loch Ness *by Patricia Lauber*	28
7	The Great Brain at the Academy *by John D. Fitzgerald*	32
8	Battle of the Ballot	36
9	From the Mixed-Up Files of Mrs. Basil E. Frankweiler *by E. L. Konigsburg*	40
10	We're Having Our Say	44
11	Mom, You're Fired *by Nancy K. Robinson*	48
12	We Live in Mexico *by Carlos Somonte*	52
13	The Last Voyage of the S.S. Edmund Fitzgerald	56
14	James and the Giant Peach *by Roald Dahl*	60
15	Little House in the Big Woods *by Laura Ingalls Wilder*	64
16	Racing on the Wind *by Edward and Ruth S. Radlauer*	68
17	Henry Reed's Journey *by Keith Robertson*	72
18	The Boston Marathon	76

19 The Good-Guy Cake
by Barbara Dillon 80

20 All About Tarantulas 84

21 The Enormous Egg
by Oliver Butterworth 88

22 Mount Washington: Small but Deadly 92

23 Paul Bunyan and His Boyhood
by Dell J. McCormick 96

24 Birth of an Island
by Millicent E. Selsam 100

25 Iditarod: The Last Great Race on Earth 104

26 Triangle of Fear
by Henry and Melissa Billings 108

27 The Man and the Snake
by Ambrose Bierce 112

28 To See Half the World
by Edward Fry 116

29 Hotel for Dogs
by Lois Duncan 120

30 Set Your Sails for Fun
by Jennifer Albert 124

Words-per-Minute Table 130

Graphs

Reading Speed 131

Comprehension 132

Critical Thinking 133

Vocabulary 134

How Am I Doing?

Lessons 1–10 135

Lessons 11–20 136

Lessons 21–30 137

To the Student

You probably talk at an average rate of 150 words a minute. But if you are a reader of average ability, you read at the rate of 250 words a minute. So your reading speed is already nearly twice as fast as your speaking or listening speed. This example shows that reading is one of the fastest ways to put verbal information into your mind.

The following chart illustrates what an increase in reading speed can do for you.

It shows the number of books read over a period of 10 years by various types of readers. Compare the number of books read by a slow reader and the number read by a fast reader.

Reading Drills is for students who want to read faster and with greater understanding. By completing the 30 lessons—reading the selections and doing the exercises—you will certainly increase

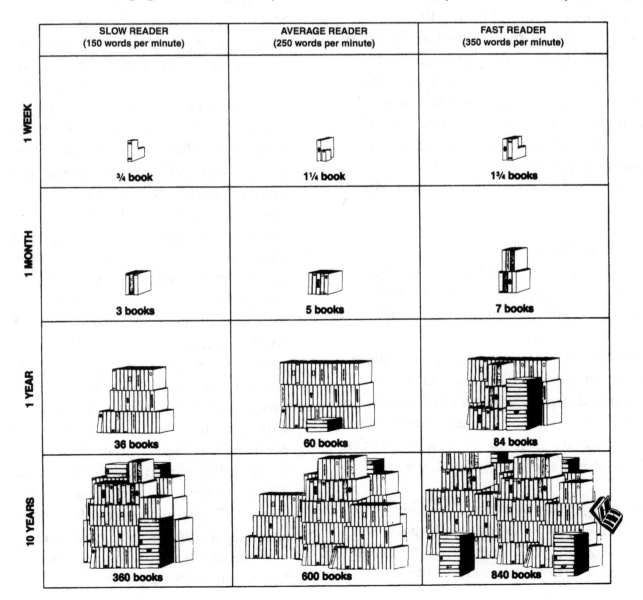

	SLOW READER (150 words per minute)	AVERAGE READER (250 words per minute)	FAST READER (350 words per minute)
1 WEEK	¾ book	1¼ book	1¾ books
1 MONTH	3 books	5 books	7 books
1 YEAR	36 books	60 books	84 books
10 YEARS	360 books	600 books	840 books

your reading speed, improve your reading comprehension, and sharpen your critical-thinking skills.

How to Use This Book

About the Book

Reading Drills, Introductory Level contains 30 lessons. Each lesson begins with a fiction or nonfiction reading selection. The lesson also includes exercises in reading comprehension, critical thinking, and vocabulary, as well as personal response questions. The reading comprehension and vocabulary exercises help you understand the selection. The critical-thinking exercises help you reflect on what you have read and how the material relates to your own experience. At the end of the lesson, the personal response questions give you the opportunity to respond to various aspects of the story or article.

The Sample Lesson

The first lesson in the book is a sample lesson that your class or group will work through together. It helps you understand how the lessons are organized. The sample lesson explains how to complete the exercises and score your answers. Sample answers and scores are printed in lighter type. If you have any questions about completing the exercises or scoring them, this is the time to get the answers.

Working Through Each Lesson

1. Begin each lesson by reading the introduction. It prepares you to read the selection. As you read the selection itself, you are timed. Either you or your teacher will set a timer when you begin reading the selection. When you finish reading, record your time on the Reading Time line in the box at the end of the selection. Then find your reading speed on the Words-per-Minute table on page 130 and record it on the Reading Speed line in the box. Finally, record your speed on the Reading Speed graph at the end of the book. Keeping track of your reading speed will help you monitor your progress.

2. Next complete the exercises. The directions for each exercise tell you how to mark your answers. When you have completed all four exercises, use the answer key provided by your teacher to check your work. Record your scores after each exercise. Then fill in your scores on the appropriate progress graphs at the back of the book. Your teacher will help you interpret your progress on the graphs.

3. Check your progress. To get the most benefit from working through these lessons, you need to take charge of your own progress in improving your comprehension, critical-thinking, and vocabulary skills. The graphs and charts help you keep track of your progress, but you need to study them from time to time to see whether your progress is satisfactory or whether you need additional work on some skills. The How Am I Doing? questions on pages 135–137 provide guidelines to help you assess your progress and determine what types of exercises you are having difficulty with.

Sample

Dowsing: Fact or Fiction?

Dowsers claim they can find water or hidden objects under the ground with a Y-shaped stick. Scientists have been trying to find out if dowsing really works and, if so, how.

Ray Burbank was having trouble finding an underground water pipe. So he asked a friend named Henry Gross for help. Gross took a Y-shaped twig and held it in his hands. Then he walked back and forth over the ground. "The pipe's right here," Gross said at last, marking the spot with a wooden stake.

Meanwhile, the water company had sent its own men to find the pipe. When the men saw Gross with the twig, they broke out laughing. Still, even though they used fancy machines, they couldn't find the pipe. The next day, Ray Burbank dug up the spot Gross had marked. Sure enough, there was the water pipe.

Gross found the pipe by using the age-old art of dowsing. Dowsers claim they can find water and other hidden things under the earth. They simply walk over the ground while holding a forked stick or rod. Suddenly, they say, the stick or rod will tremble in the dowser's hands. It will point down toward what is hidden below the ground. When asked what makes the stick move, many dowsers shrug. "I don't know how it works," they say. "It just does."

Dowsing goes back at least to the 16th century. That's when the first written account of it appeared in Germany. In those days, dowsing was used to find precious metals. The practice spread throughout Europe, and, later, the United States. People in Asia and Africa also began to practice dowsing.

Some of today's dowsers have a pretty good record of success. One of the very best dowsers is Hans Schroter. He has picked sites for hundreds of wells. In fact, he has chosen 691 spots. Only 27 of these have failed to yield water.

Still, the question remains: How do dowsers do it? What could make a stick suddenly bend down toward something far underground? Is there some force in nature at work? Some people believe each hidden object must send out some kind of mysterious wave. Water, too, must send out waves. Dowsers, then, are people sensitive enough to pick up these waves.

Some scientists believe that dowsers' success stories are just a matter of luck. Others have another theory. It's not the stick that helps a dowser, they say. It's the dowser's own knowledge of the land. Dowsers often know the land they are walking very well. So they might pick up clues without even realizing it. They might see that underground water changes the look of the soil in a certain area. The shape of the ground might offer hints. Geologist Jay Lehr says that experienced dowsers are often experts in picking up such clues.

Still, a few experts have decided that dowsing is for real. One is the German

4

scientist Hans-Dieter Betz. In 1995, Betz wrote a report on dowsing declaring that good dowsers can indeed detect water below the ground. So far, though, most scientists are not convinced.

So that puts us back where we started. Is dowsing fact or fiction? ■

✔ Enter your reading time below. Then look up your reading speed on the Words-per-Minute table on page 130.

Reading Time _____

Reading Speed _____

Enter your reading speed on the Reading Speed graph on Page 131.

Comprehension

Put an **X** in the box next to the correct answer for each question or statement. Do not look back at the selection.

1. When the water company men saw the dowser Ray Burbank hired, they
   - ☐ a. asked him for help.
   - ☒ b. laughed at him.
   - ☐ c. made him leave the land.

2. Dowsers find things underground by
   - ☐ a. closing their eyes and thinking hard.
   - ☐ b. listening to the sound a forked stick makes.
   - ☒ c. walking over ground with a forked stick.

3. When the forked stick is held over a buried object, the stick
   - ☐ a. jumps out of the dowser's hand.
   - ☐ b. becomes hot.
   - ☒ c. bends down toward the ground.

4. From where did the first written account of dowsing come?
   - ☒ a. Germany
   - ☐ b. United States
   - ☐ c. Asia

5. Dowsing was first used to find
   - ☐ a. water.
   - ☐ b. buried treasure.
   - ☒ c. precious metals.

6. One of the very best dowsers is
   - ☒ a. Hans Schroter.
   - ☐ b. Ray Burbank.
   - ☐ c. Hans-Dieter Betz.

7. Some scientists believe that dowsers' success is due to
   - ☐ a. hard work.
   - ☒ b. luck.
   - ☐ c. expert training.

8. Most scientists are convinced that
   - ☐ a. good dowsers can detect water below ground.
   - ☒ b. dowsing does not really work.
   - ☐ c. they can learn much from good dowsers.

✎ ___8___ Number of correct answers
Enter this number on the Comprehension graph on page 132.

Critical Thinking

Put an ☒ in the box next to the best answer for each question or statement. You may look back at the selection if you'd like.

1. The author's main purpose was to
   - ☒ a. inform you about dowsing.
   - ☐ b. instruct you how to dowse
   - ☐ c. entertain you with explanations of an unusual practice.

2. Which statement best expresses the main idea of the selection?
   - ☐ a. Dowsing is a good way to find hidden objects.
   - ☐ b. Dowsers use a forked stick or a rod that trembles when it is placed over a buried object.
   - ☒ c. Dowsing seems to be a combination of art, skill, and luck.

3. Based on the selection, you can conclude that
   - ☐ a. most dowsers have studied rocks and earth in college.
   - ☒ b. an advantage of dowsing is that it can be done with cheap tools.
   - ☐ c. if scientists don't believe in a practice, everyone gives that practice up.

4. Which of the following is the best description of dowsing?
   - ☐ a. a reliable method of finding things underground
   - ☐ b. an ancient, mysterious practice not to be taken seriously
   - ☒ c. a practice that has a pretty good record of success, but is still considered unreliable

5. A dowser's stick might suddenly bend downward because of
   - ☒ a. mysterious waves.
   - ☐ b. a magnetic force.
   - ☐ c. underground pipes.

6. Which of the following is a statement of opinion rather than fact?
   - ☐ a. Dowsing goes back to at least the 16th century.
   - ☒ b. It's not the stick that helps a dowser; it's the dowser's own knowledge of the land.
   - ☐ c. In 1995, Hans-Dieter Betz wrote a report on dowsing.

7. Which of the following items does *not* fit with the other two?
   - ☐ a. forked stick
   - ☒ b. water pipe
   - ☐ c. rod

8. Which of the following best summarizes this selection?
   - ☐ a. Dowsing dates back to the 16th century in Germany. It later spread throughout the world.
   - ☒ b. Dowsing is the ancient practice of using a forked stick or rod to find things underground. Most scientists are not convinced it works despite some success.
   - ☐ c. Dowsing is the practice of using a forked stick to locate underground water. The dowser walks over the ground holding the stick.

✎ ____8____ **Number of correct answers**
Enter this number on the Critical Thinking graph on page 133.

Vocabulary

Each numbered sentence contains an underlined word from the selection. Following are three definitions. Put an **X** in the box next to the best meaning of the word as it is used in the sentence.

1. Dowsers <u>claim</u> they can find water and other things hidden underground.
   - ☐ a. deny
   - ☒ b. say strongly
   - ☐ c. believe

2. Suddenly the stick or rod will <u>tremble</u> in the dowser's hand.
   - ☐ a. twist
   - ☐ b. remain steady
   - ☒ c. shake

3. In those days, dowsing was used to find <u>precious</u> metals.
   - ☒ a. valuable
   - ☐ b. beautiful
   - ☐ c. worthless

4. He has picked <u>sites</u> for hundreds of wells.
   - ☒ a. locations
   - ☐ b. workers
   - ☐ c. underground pipes

5. Only 27 of these sites have failed to <u>yield</u> water.
   - ☐ a. spray
   - ☐ b. hold back
   - ☒ c. produce

6. Others have another <u>theory</u>.
   - ☐ a. plan
   - ☒ b. explanation
   - ☐ c. hidden object

7. In 1995, Betz wrote a report stating that good dowsers can indeed <u>detect</u> water below the ground.
   - ☒ a. discover
   - ☐ b. make use of
   - ☐ c. follow

8. So far, though, most scientists are not <u>convinced</u>.
   - ☐ a. doubtful
   - ☒ b. sure
   - ☐ c. interested

✎ ___8___ **Number of correct answers Enter this number on the Vocabulary graph on page 134.**

Personal Response

What was most surprising or interesting to you about this selection?

<u>[Tell about what you felt was surprising or interesting.]</u>

_____

_____

1 | Magic Spinach

by Carol Eron and Fulang Lo

In this folk tale from China, a good son and a mean landlord both get what they deserve.

Once in a village in China there lived an old blind lady and her son. The son swore to take care of his mother, so he did not marry and lived instead in his mother's house.

In summer he took her out walking in the cool night air, and in winter he warmed her bed before she got in. Everyone knew that he was a remarkable boy.

Then one spring a flood came and covered the village farms with water. Nothing could grow anymore, and the son had to walk far to find wild grasses for them to eat.

One day while he was cutting grasses, it began to rain, so he took shelter in a nearby cave. When he sat down, he felt tender, fresh leaves under him. He saw that it was spinach and he began to cut it. No sooner had he cut the last of the leaves than new leaves sprang up. He cut these, too, and that night he carried a basketful of fresh spinach home to his mother.

The next day he returned to the cave, and it was the same as before. No matter how much spinach he cut, more grew in its place.

On the third day the son returned to the cave once again. This time he uprooted the spinach. I'll plant it in the village so that everyone might have spinach, he thought.

As he pulled up the last plant, he saw something glinting in the ground. It was a small, perfectly smooth, perfectly round stone.

He took it home with him and put it in the rice jar, where he was saving a handful of rice for his mother's birthday. The next day when he opened the jar, it was full of rice. He took some of it out, but the jar quickly filled up again. When he poured out all the rice, he was overjoyed to find that once again the jar filled itself to the very top.

The son picked up the jar and went out to share the rice with the poor families in the village. Soon everyone knew about the magic stone.

When the son returned home, he met the landlord at the door. The landlord asked him for some rice, and the son gave it. Then the landlord asked for the stone.

"No, I will give you anything but the stone," the son said, holding it tightly in his hand.

"I don't want anything else—only the stone," the landlord said. And he kicked the son in the stomach, snatched the stone, and stuck it in his mouth to keep it safe. Then the landlord ran home. But on the way he slipped and swallowed the stone.

Suddenly he felt very thirsty and drank all the water in his house. But he was still thirsty, and there was no one to bring him more water. So the landlord ran outside and started drinking the floodwaters from the ground. He drank and drank, until he drank up all the water. . . .

And then he turned into a toad. ■

✔ Enter your reading time below. Then look up your reading speed on the Words-per-Minute table on page 130.

Reading Time _____

Reading Speed _____

Enter your reading speed on the Reading Speed graph on page 131.

Comprehension

Put an X in the box next to the correct answer for each question or statement. Do not look back at the selection.

1. The son never married because
   ☐ a. he swore to take care of his blind mother.
   ☐ b. he could not find a suitable woman.
   ☐ c. he was too poor.

2. The flood that covered the farms with water came in the
   ☐ a. fall.
   ☐ b. winter.
   ☐ c. spring.

3. Why did the son seek shelter in the cave?
   ☐ a. It was getting dark.
   ☐ b. It began raining.
   ☐ c. The flood waters were rising.

4. How many days did the son visit the cave?
   ☐ a. two
   ☐ b. three
   ☐ c. four

5. What did the son find glinting in the ground in the cave?
   ☐ a. fresh leaves of spinach
   ☐ b. a small, round stone
   ☐ c. a bowl of rice

6. When the landlord came to the door, the son gave him
   ☐ a. some spinach.
   ☐ b. the magic stone.
   ☐ c. some rice.

7. The landlord stuck the stone in his mouth in order to
   ☐ a. keep it safe.
   ☐ b. keep it from drying out.
   ☐ c. make it easier for him to carry.

8. What happened because the landlord swallowed the stone?
   ☐ a. He died.
   ☐ b. He turned into a toad.
   ☐ c. The stone lost its magic power.

✎ _____ Number of correct answers
Enter this number on the Comprehension graph on page 132.

Critical Thinking

Put an **X** in the box next to the best answer for each question or statement. You may look back at the selection if you'd like.

1. Which statement below describes the type of story "Magic Spinach" is?
   - ☐ a. a story made up long ago about brave heroes and gods with special powers
   - ☐ b. a story made up long ago about a good, hardworking character
   - ☐ c. a story of a real person's life told by that person

2. The authors tell this story mainly by
   - ☐ a. retelling a story that has been told before.
   - ☐ b. using their own imaginations.
   - ☐ c. retelling their own personal experiences.

3. Another good title for this story is
   - ☐ a. "The Blind Lady and Her Son."
   - ☐ b. "The Miracle that Saved a Village."
   - ☐ c. "Greed Receives Its Just Reward."

4. How did the landlord probably find out about the magic stone?
   - ☐ a. He saw the son with it.
   - ☐ b. The son told him.
   - ☐ c. One of the poor villagers told him.

5. Nothing could grow on the village farms because
   - ☐ a. a flood had covered the farms with water.
   - ☐ b. the farmers had no seeds.
   - ☐ c. the soil had dried out from lack of rain.

6. Which event happened last?
   - ☐ a. The son carried home a basketful of fresh spinach.
   - ☐ b. The son found a round stone in the cave.
   - ☐ c. A flood covered the village farms with water.

7. Which word best describes the son?
   - ☐ a. self-sacrificing
   - ☐ b. honest
   - ☐ c. strong

8. The landlord wanted the magic stone so he could
   - ☐ a. use its powers to help the poor.
   - ☐ b. use it to help only himself.
   - ☐ c. keep it safe for the son and his blind mother.

✎ _____ **Number of correct answers** Enter this number on the Critical Thinking graph on page 133.

Vocabulary

Each numbered sentence contains an underlined word or phrase from the selection. Following are three definitions. Put an **X** in the box next to the best meaning of the word as it is used in the sentence.

1. The son <u>swore</u> to take care of his mother.
   - ☐ a. refused
   - ☐ b. promised
   - ☐ c. agreed

2. Everyone knew that he was a
   <u>remarkable</u> boy.
   - ☐ a. very smart
   - ☐ b. selfish
   - ☐ c. unusual

3. One day while he was cutting grasses, it
   began to rain, so he took <u>shelter</u> in a
   nearby cave.
   - ☐ a. a raincoat
   - ☐ b. protection
   - ☐ c. caution

4. When he sat down, he felt <u>tender</u>,
   fresh leaves under him.
   - ☐ a. mild
   - ☐ b. rough
   - ☐ c. soft

5. No sooner had he cut the last of the
   leaves than new leaves <u>sprang up</u>.
   - ☐ a. fell off
   - ☐ b. grew
   - ☐ c. died

6. This time he <u>uprooted</u> the spinach.
   - ☐ a. removed completely
   - ☐ b. covered up
   - ☐ c. planted

7. As he pulled up the last plant, he saw
   something <u>glinting</u> in the ground.
   - ☐ a. growing
   - ☐ b. shining
   - ☐ c. stuck

8. And he kicked the son in the stomach,
   <u>snatched</u> the stone, and stuck it in his
   mouth to keep it safe.
   - ☐ a. grabbed suddenly
   - ☐ b. borrowed
   - ☐ c. threw away

✎ _____ **Number of correct answers**
**Enter this number on the Vocabulary
graph on page 134.**

Personal Response

Using four or five sentences, write a different ending to the story. Begin at the moment
the landlord swallows the stone.

_____

_____

_____

Name one thing you would do with the magic stone if you found it.

_____

_____

_____

2 | The Year Without a Summer

It was cold and snow covered the ground in New England. This is not unusual weather for this area in the late fall or winter. But this was summer! What was going on in the year without a summer?

It was 1816, and the spring in New England was cold and damp. The farmers grumbled a bit because their crop planting was delayed. Such chilly springs in New England, however, are not unusual. Anyone who takes up farming in that part of the United States has to expect the worst. But even the old hands were not prepared for the summer of 1816.

June started out nice and warm. It made the farmers forget the frosts and snows of May. But on June 6, and for the next five days, snow and hail returned. Several inches of snow covered the newly planted fields. It was so cold that a fire was necessary to keep warm indoors. It felt like mid-November rather than early June. People had to wear winter hats and coats.

Finally, more normal weather returned. The farmers tried to repair the damage done by the killing frost and snow. In July, however, a second blast of cold arrived. It was not as severe as the June cold, but this was July, and July was supposed to be the hottest month of the year. Ice and cold again killed the crops. From July 5 to July 9 the temperature hovered near the freezing mark.

Warm, summerlike weather finally came on July 12. The weather stayed pleasant until August 20. Around this time the farmers began to harvest those crops that had survived the cold spells of June

and July. Then came the most incredible cold of all. Frost again killed crops in New Hampshire and Maine. The mountains of Vermont were covered with snow. In fact, it snowed every month that year in Vermont. The corn crop was ruined. In Canada, even the normally hardy wheat crop was wiped out.

The story was the same in Europe. Crop failures and food shortages plagued the people. Record-cold temperatures were recorded. Unseasonable snows fell. In the years to come, 1816 would be known as "The Year Without a Summer."

What caused this frigid summer with the strangely colored sky? Scientists blame the volcanic eruption of Mt. Tambora, in Indonesia—half the world away. The explosion was so great that the height of this volcanic mountain was reduced by 5,000 feet. Many cubic miles of ash and dust were hurled into the air. They gathered into a huge cloud in the upper atmosphere. This cloud then began to circle the globe. It prevented some of the sun's rays from reaching Earth. It also caused some spectacular sunsets and weird colors in the sky.

No one is certain just how much blame belongs to Tambora for the unusually cold summer of 1816. Some of the cold might have been the result of normal weather changes. But other volcanoes, such as Krakatoa in 1883 and Gunung Agung in 1963, have also been accused of causing unusual weather. In 1982, El Chichon in southern Mexico exploded. Many scientists believe that its impact on world weather will be felt for many years to come. ■

✔ Enter your reading time below. Then look up your reading speed on the Words-per-Minute table on page 130.

Reading Time _____

Reading Speed _____

Enter your reading speed on the Reading Speed graph on page 131.

Comprehension

Put an **X** in the box next to the correct answer for each question or statement. Do not look back at the selection.

1. The year without a summer was
   - ☐ a. 1883.
   - ☐ b. 1816.
   - ☐ c. 1963.

2. During the first few days of June that year, New England weather was
   - ☐ a. cold and snowy.
   - ☐ b. chilly and cloudy.
   - ☐ c. sunny and warm.

3. The hottest month in New England is supposed to be
   - ☐ a. June.
   - ☐ b. July.
   - ☐ c. August.

4. In the year without a summer, snow fell every month in
   - ☐ a. Vermont.
   - ☐ b. New Hampshire.
   - ☐ c. Europe.

5. The normally hardy wheat crop was wiped out in
   - ☐ a. Canada.
   - ☐ b. Maine.
   - ☐ c. New Hampshire

6. What did scientists blame for the unusual cold of that summer?
   - ☐ a. a volcanic eruption
   - ☐ b. an earthquake
   - ☐ c. normal weather changes

7. Where is Mt. Tambora located?
   - ☐ a. New England
   - ☐ b. Canada
   - ☐ c. Indonesia

8. Krakatoa and El Chichon are
   - ☐ a. cities in Europe.
   - ☐ b. towns in Mexico.
   - ☐ c. volcanoes.

✎ _____ **Number of correct answers**
Enter this number on the Comprehension graph on page 132.

Critical Thinking

Put an **X** in the box next to the best answer for each question or statement. You may look back at the selection if you'd like.

1. The author probably wrote this selection to
   - ☐ a. inform you about farming in New England.
   - ☐ b. explain how major events, such as volcanic explosions, can affect weather.
   - ☐ c. warn you that volcanoes are dangerous.

2. Which of the following statements best expresses the main idea of the selection?
   - ☐ a. During the cold summer of 1816, the corn crop was ruined.
   - ☐ b. Scientists believe that volcanic ash and dust from Mt. Tambora may have caused the cold and snow in the summer of 1816.
   - ☐ c. Unusual weather can result from the explosion of a volcano.

3. Compared to other parts of the country, the length of the growing season in New England is
   - ☐ a. about the same.
   - ☐ b. longer.
   - ☐ c. shorter.

4. Which of the following statements from the selection best describes the summer of 1816?
   - ☐ a. Ice and snow again killed the crops.
   - ☐ b. Warm, summerlike weather finally came on July 12.
   - ☐ c. The weather stayed pleasant until August 20.

5. A cloud of ashes and dust from the volcanic eruption of Mt. Tambora
   - ☐ a. prevented some of the sun's rays from reaching Earth.
   - ☐ b. reduced the height of the volcanic mountain by 5,000 feet.
   - ☐ c. started several tornadoes.

6. Which of the following is a statement of opinion rather than fact?
   - ☐ a. In 1982, El Chichon in southern Mexico exploded.
   - ☐ b. Frost again killed the crops in New Hampshire and Maine.
   - ☐ c. Anyone who takes up farming in that part of the United States has to expect the worst.

7. In what way were June and November alike in 1816?
   - ☐ a. Both months were unusually warm.
   - ☐ b. Crop planting was delayed in both months.
   - ☐ c. Both months were cold and snow covered the ground.

8. Which of the following does *not* fit with the other two?
   - ☐ a. Maine
   - ☐ b. Vermont
   - ☐ c. Canada

✎ _____ **Number of correct answers**
Enter this number on the Critical Thinking graph on page 133.

Vocabulary

Each numbered sentence contains an underlined word from the selection. Following are three definitions. Put an **X** in the box next to the best meaning of the word as it is used in the sentence.

1. The farmers grumbled a bit because their crop planting was <u>delayed</u>.
   - ☐ a. put off till later
   - ☐ b. to be done sooner
   - ☐ c. mostly ruined

2. It was not as <u>severe</u> as the June cold, but this was July.
   - ☐ a. mild
   - ☐ b. expected
   - ☐ c. harsh

3. Around this time the farmers began to harvest those crops that survived the cold <u>spells</u> of June and July.
   - ☐ a. periods of time
   - ☐ b. magic powers
   - ☐ c. planting season

4. Crop failures and food shortages <u>plagued</u> the people.
   - ☐ a. caused to be sick
   - ☐ b. greatly interested
   - ☐ c. greatly troubled

5. The explosion was so great that the height of this volcanic mountain was <u>reduced</u> by 5,000 feet.
   - ☐ a. increased
   - ☐ b. lowered
   - ☐ c. broken up

6. This cloud then began to circle the globe. It <u>prevented</u> some of the sun's rays from reaching Earth.
   - ☐ a. slowed down
   - ☐ b. stopped
   - ☐ c. brightened

7. It also caused some spectacular sunsets and <u>weird</u> colors in the sky.
   - ☐ a. unusual
   - ☐ b. bright
   - ☐ c. mysterious

8. Many scientists believe that its <u>impact</u> on world weather will be felt for many years to come.
   - ☐ a. effect
   - ☐ b. crashing
   - ☐ c. disturbing

✎ _____ **Number of correct answers**
Enter this number on the Vocabulary graph on page 134.

Personal Response

What was most surprising or interesting to you about this selection?

_____

_____

What new question do you have about this topic?

_____

_____

3 | The Three Brothers and the Treasure

by José Maria Eça de Queiroz

In this passage from a story from Portugal, three poor brothers find a great treasure. Do they trust each other to share it equally?

Years ago, in Portugal, there lived three brothers. Their names were Rui, Pablo, and Miguel. They were the laziest, most worthless young men in their village.

The brothers lived in an old house made of clay. One winter day there was a terrible storm. The storm destroyed the roof of the house. It broke all the windows. The brothers had no money to fix the house. So they stayed in their freezing kitchen all winter.

When night came, the brothers ate a meal of black bread. Then they made their way through the snow to the stable. They slept there in the straw. During the night they heard wolves howling outside. The brothers were very poor. And their poverty made them fiercer than the wolves.

Finally spring came. One morning the brothers got on their mules. They rode into the woods. They were hoping to catch some rabbits for food. Or maybe they could find some fruit. It would taste good with the black bread.

Suddenly the brothers came upon a cave. The cave was carved into a large rock. It was hard to see the cave because the rock was concealed by thick bushes.

The brothers pulled out their knives. They cut through the bushes. Then they entered the cave. Inside the cave they saw an old iron chest. The chest had three locks. And in each lock was a key.

The brothers quickly opened the locks. They threw open the chest. They saw that the chest was filled with pieces of gold!

The brothers were delighted when they saw this treasure. They laughed. They shouted. They danced wildly about.

Finally, they faced one another. They did not speak. But their looks seemed to say, "What shall we do with this gold?"

Rui was the oldest of the three. He said, "Brothers, we must divide this gold equally."

Pablo and Miguel thought that was fair. Rui said, "But this chest is very heavy. We cannot move it now. We have not eaten all day."

Rui turned to Pablo. He was the youngest of the three. Rui said, "Take one piece of gold. Put it in your pocket. Ride into town. Buy three large leather bags to carry the gold. Buy three loaves of bread and three pieces of meat. Buy three bottles of wine. When you return, we will eat. Then we will take home the gold."

Pablo stood looking down at the shining gold. He did not move. Finally he said, "The chest has three parts. Each part locks with a different key. I will lock my part. And I will take my key with me."

"Then I will lock my part of the chest too," said Miguel. "And I will keep the key."

"And I will do the same thing," said Rui.

So each brother locked his part of the chest. And each put the key safely in his pocket.

Pablo was satisfied. He said good-bye. As he rode away, Miguel and Rui could hear him singing. ■

✔ Enter your reading time below. Then look up your reading speed on the Words-per-Minute table on page 130.

    Reading Time   _____

    Reading Speed   _____
Enter your reading speed on the Reading Speed graph on page 131.

Comprehension

Put an **X** in the box next to the correct answer for each question or statement. Do not look back at the selection.

1. The brothers' old house was made of
   ☐ a. clay.
   ☐ b. logs.
   ☐ c. mud and grass.

2. The brothers' house was badly damaged by
   ☐ a. a tornado.
   ☐ b. an earthquake.
   ☐ c. a winter storm.

3. The brothers could not fix their house because
   ☐ a. it was too badly damaged.
   ☐ b. they had no money.
   ☐ c. they did not know how.

4. Why did the brothers ride their mules into the woods?
   ☐ a. to gather firewood
   ☐ b. to get food
   ☐ c. to cut timber with which to repair their house

5. The brothers discovered a cave that was
   ☐ a. carved into a large rock.
   ☐ b. on the side of a mountain.
   ☐ c. under their house.

6. It was hard to see the cave at first because it
   ☐ a. was nighttime.
   ☐ b. was concealed by thick bushes.
   ☐ c. had a very small entrance.

7. What did the brothers discover in the cave?
   ☐ a. a chest filled with diamonds
   ☐ b. a chest filled with gold pieces
   ☐ c. a chest containing a treasure map

8. Before trying to move the chest, the brothers decided to
   ☐ a. sleep.
   ☐ b. bury some of the treasure.
   ☐ c. eat.

✎ _____ **Number of correct answers**
Enter this number on the Comprehension graph on page 132.

Critical Thinking

Put an **X** in the box next to the best answer for each question or statement. You may look back at the selection if you'd like.

1. The author's purpose in writing this selection was to
   - ☐ a. describe life in a poor village in Portugal.
   - ☐ b. express an opinion about lazy people.
   - ☐ c. entertain you with an interesting story.

2. Who is telling this story?
   - ☐ a. the brother Rui
   - ☐ b. an outside observer
   - ☐ c. the brother Pablo

3. You can conclude that the leader among the brothers is
   - ☐ a. Rui.
   - ☐ b. Pablo.
   - ☐ c. Miguel.

4. Based on what you've read, you can predict that the three brothers will probably
   - ☐ a. trust each other to be fair.
   - ☐ b. fight among themselves.
   - ☐ c. decide to leave the treasure in the cave.

5. Pablo decided to take his key with him after locking his part of the chest because he
   - ☐ a. was afraid his brothers would lose the key.
   - ☐ b. wanted to have a copy of the key made in the village.
   - ☐ c. did not trust his brothers.

6. Which of the following is a statement of opinion rather than fact?
   - ☐ a. Years ago, in Portugal, there lived three brothers. Their names were Rui, Pablo, and Miguel.
   - ☐ b. The brothers lived in an old house made of clay.
   - ☐ c. They were the laziest, most worthless young men in their village.

7. Why do you think Pablo had to ride into town to get food instead of Rui or Miguel?
   - ☐ a. He was the youngest.
   - ☐ b. He knew the way.
   - ☐ c. He was the smartest.

8. Which event happened last?
   - ☐ a. The brothers discovered a hidden cave.
   - ☐ b. The brothers' house was badly damaged.
   - ☐ c. During the night they heard wolves howling outside.

✎ _____ **Number of correct answers**
Enter this number on the Critical Thinking graph on page 133.

Vocabulary

Each numbered sentence contains an underlined word from the selection. Following are three definitions. Put an **X** in the box next to the best meaning of the word as it is used in the sentence.

1. They were the laziest, most <u>worthless</u> young men in their village.
   - ☐ a. useless
   - ☐ b. tireless
   - ☐ c. careless

2. The storm <u>destroyed</u> the roof of the house.
   - ☐ a. ruined
   - ☐ b. repaired
   - ☐ c. saved

3. And their poverty made them <u>fiercer</u> than wolves.
   - ☐ a. smarter
   - ☐ b. poorer
   - ☐ c. wilder

4. The cave was <u>carved</u> into a large rock.
   - ☐ a. chopped
   - ☐ b. made
   - ☐ c. cut

5. It was hard to see the cave because the rock was <u>concealed</u> by thick bushes.
   - ☐ a. surrounded
   - ☐ b. hidden
   - ☐ c. made known

6. The brothers were <u>delighted</u> when they saw this treasure.
   - ☐ a. amused
   - ☐ b. disappointed
   - ☐ c. very glad

7. He said, "Brothers, we must divide this gold <u>equally</u>."
   - ☐ a. quickly
   - ☐ b. fairly
   - ☐ c. quietly

8. Pablo was <u>satisfied</u>.
   - ☐ a. pleased
   - ☐ b. worried
   - ☐ c. angered

✎ _____ **Number of correct answers**
Enter this number on the Vocabulary graph on page 134.

Personal Response

In five to eight sentences, write your own ending to this story.

_____

_____

_____

_____

_____

4 | How to Lasso a Shark

by William B. McMorris

Would you like to put on scuba gear, jump into the ocean, and try to catch a hungry shark? If you would, you might like to join the author and his friends who do just that. In this article, he tells you how they do it.

Start as if you were going to build a big butterfly net. The handle needs to be about 10 feet long. The rigid hoop is about three feet across. Instead of a net, you string a noose around the inside of the hoop with spring clips. Now, if you are like Trevor Long, associate director of Sea World near Brisbane, Australia, you are ready to hunt sharks. Trevor gets a couple of friends, puts on his scuba gear, and takes this big hoop with a rope on it down 85 feet in the sea.

The divers go to a place where a narrow channel about 30 feet deep cuts through a reef. At special times of the year, huge schools of little fish called pilchard whirl through. They are followed by hungry yellowtail kingfish that are followed by hungry sharks.

When a shark swims by, Trevor slips the hoop over the fish's head and jerks the rope tight. Another diver gets the handle and hoop out of the way, and the third helps hold the rope. At this point, two men have roped a very large fish with very large teeth.

Why doesn't the shark whirl around and make a meal of the seagoing cowboy? "They almost always swim away," Trevor says.

After a battle of about 20 minutes, the shark usually gives up. The fish blows out some air bubbles and goes limp. This is a sign it is safe to bring it to the surface. If the fish is brought up too quickly, a sudden change in pressure may kill it.

"When they get to the top they get more life," Trevor warns. "They bite the motors, the boat, and anything else that comes in contact."

He adds quickly, "We're on the boat at this time." The crew leads the fish into a sling, winches it into a tank on board, and they run for home. Home is a 110,000-gallon tank in Sea World's Theatre of the Sea.

Sea World divers put on as many as 11 shows per day about the history of diving. Audiences seated in the air-conditioned theater watch through a six-inch-thick wall of clear acrylic. It's easy to think of the fish as almost tame, just big pets in a giant aquarium. But they are not.

Sharks can fool even experts. A horrified audience watched one afternoon as a six-foot-long bronze whaler shark tore at a diver's leg for several seconds before the man could be rescued. It happened, Trevor said, after thousands of trouble-free shows. Nobody can be sure just why the attack took place.

The diver lived, the fish was replaced, but bronze whalers are watched very carefully any time a man is in the water.

Trevor credits the Boy Scouts for helping him in his career. "Our

Scoutmaster let us solve all kinds of outdoor living problems by ourselves. He also insisted we be good with knots. I've applied both skills many times above and beneath the water."

These skills are especially useful when he sets up the loop of a rope that lassos sharks. ■

✔ Enter your reading time below. Then look up your reading speed on the Words-per-Minute table on page 130.

Reading Time _____

Reading Speed _____

Enter your reading speed on the Reading Speed graph on page 131.

Comprehension

Put an **X** in the box next to the correct answer for each question or statement. Do not look back at the selection.

1. The handle of the shark lasso should be
   ☐ a. 85 feet long.
   ☐ b. 30 feet long.
   ☐ c. 10 feet long.

2. Trevor Long works with sharks in
   ☐ a. America.
   ☐ b. Australia.
   ☐ c. Brazil.

3. To lasso a shark in the sea, Trevor Long needs
   ☐ a. one helper.
   ☐ b. two helpers.
   ☐ c. three helpers.

4. Before giving up, a roped shark usually battles for about
   ☐ a. 16 minutes.
   ☐ b. 20 minutes.
   ☐ c. 30 minutes.

5. When the shark blows out air bubbles and goes limp, it is a sign that it is
   ☐ a. safe to bring it to the surface.
   ☐ b. very dangerous to handle.
   ☐ c. probably dead.

6. When sharks get to the surface, they
   ☐ a. try to swim away.
   ☐ b. stop battling.
   ☐ c. bite anything they come in contact with.

7. What kind of shark attacked a diver?
   ☐ a. a great white
   ☐ b. a yellowtail
   ☐ c. a bronze whaler

8. Whom does Trevor Long credit for helping him in his career?
   ☐ a. the Boy Scouts
   ☐ b. shark experts
   ☐ c. his diving friends

✎ _____ Number of correct answers
Enter this number on the Comprehension graph on page 132.

Critical Thinking

Put an **X** in the box next to the best answer for each question or statement. You may look back at the selection if you'd like.

1. The author's main purpose in writing the article was to describe
   - ☐ a. Sea World's Theatre of the Sea.
   - ☐ b. one way to catch a shark.
   - ☐ c. how to use scuba gear.

2. Which is the most important idea in the article?
   - ☐ a. Sharks are a popular attraction at Sea World.
   - ☐ b. Sharks are very difficult to catch.
   - ☐ c. Nobody can predict how sharks will act.

3. Trevor Long captures sharks for the purpose of
   - ☐ a. scientific study.
   - ☐ b. providing food.
   - ☐ c. entertaining people.

4. The first thing Trevor Long does when he hunts sharks is to
   - ☐ a. make a hoop with a noose inside.
   - ☐ b. get a couple of friends to help.
   - ☐ c. put on his scuba gear.

5. What could happen if a shark is brought to the surface too quickly?
   - ☐ a. It could escape.
   - ☐ b. It could die.
   - ☐ c. It could attack divers.

6. Which of the following is a statement of opinion rather than fact?
   - ☐ a. Sea World divers put on as many as 11 shows per day.
   - ☐ b. It's easy to think of the sharks as almost tame.
   - ☐ c. Sharks can fool even experts.

7. The author thinks it's easy to think a shark is like a
   - ☐ a. big pet.
   - ☐ b. yellowtail kingfish.
   - ☐ c. pilchard.

8. Which of the following does *not* fit with the other two?
   - ☐ a. shark
   - ☐ b. pilchard
   - ☐ c. aquarium

✎ _____ **Number of correct answers**
Enter this number on the Critical Thinking graph on page 133.

Vocabulary

Each numbered sentence contains an underlined word from the selection. Following are three definitions. Put an **X** in the box next to the best meaning of the word as it is used in the sentence.

1. The <u>rigid</u> hoop is about three feet across.
   - ☐ a. stiff
   - ☐ b. knitted
   - ☐ c. diving

2. A narrow <u>channel</u> about 30 feet deep cuts through a reef.
   - ☐ a. wave
   - ☐ b. river
   - ☐ c. passage

3. Why doesn't the shark <u>whirl</u> around and make a meal of the seagoing cowboy?
   - ☐ a. twist
   - ☐ b. growl
   - ☐ c. bite

4. The fish blows out some bubbles and goes <u>limp</u>.
   - ☐ a. down
   - ☐ b. relaxed
   - ☐ c. quickly

5. They bite the motors, the boat, and anything else that comes in <u>contact</u>.
   - ☐ a. movement
   - ☐ b. touch
   - ☐ c. noise

6. Sharks even can fool <u>experts</u>.
   - ☐ a. people who investigate situations
   - ☐ b. people who train animals
   - ☐ c. people who know all about a subject

7. A <u>horrified</u> audience watched one afternoon as a six-foot-long bronze whaler shark tore at a diver's leg for several seconds.
   - ☐ a. fascinated
   - ☐ b. shocked
   - ☐ c. surprised

8. I've <u>applied</u> both skills many times above and beneath the water.
   - ☐ a. taught
   - ☐ b. learned
   - ☐ c. used

✎ _____ Number of correct answers
Enter this number on the Vocabulary graph on page 134.

Personal Response

What was most surprising or interesting to you about this article?

_____

_____

_____

If you could ask the author of this article one question, what would it be?

_____

_____

_____

5 | Tuck Everlasting

by Natalie Babbitt

In this passage Winnie is approached by a mysterious stranger. Who is he? What does he want?

At sunset of that same long day, a stranger came strolling up the road from the village and paused at the Fosters' gate. Winnie was once again in the yard, this time intent on catching fireflies, and at first she didn't notice him. But, after a few moments of watching her, he called out, "Good evening!"

He was remarkably tall and narrow, this stranger standing there. His long chin faded off into a thin, apologetic beard, but his suit was a jaunty yellow that seemed to glow a little in the fading light. A black hat dangled from one hand, and as Winnie came toward him, he passed the other through his dry, gray hair, settling it smoothly. "Well, now," he said in a light voice. "Out for fireflies, are you?"

"Yes," said Winnie.

"A lovely thing to do on a summer evening," said the man richly. "A lovely entertainment. I used to do it myself when I was your age. But of course that was a long, long time ago." He laughed, gesturing in self-deprecation with long, thin fingers. His tall body moved continuously; a foot tapped, a shoulder twitched. And it moved in angles, rather jerkily. But at the same time he had a kind of grace, like a well-handled marionette. Indeed he seemed almost to hang suspended there in the twilight. But Winnie, though she was half-charmed, was suddenly reminded of the stiff black ribbons that had hung on the door of the cottage for her grandfather's funeral. She frowned and looked at the man more closely. But his smile seemed perfectly all right, quite agreeable and friendly. "Is this your house?" asked the man, folding his arms now and leaning against the gate.

"Yes," said Winnie. "We've lived here forever."

"Forever," the man echoed thoughtfully.

It was not a question, but Winnie decided to explain anyway. "Well, not forever, of course, but as long as there've been any people here. My grandmother was born here. She says this was all trees once, just one big forest everywhere around, but it's mostly all cut down now. Except for the wood."

"I see," said the man, pulling at his beard. "So of course you know everyone, and everything that goes on."

"Well, not especially," said Winnie. "At least, *I* don't. Why?"

The man lifted his eyebrows. "Oh," he said, "I'm looking for someone. A family."

"I don't know anybody much," said Winnie, with a shrug. "But my father might. You could ask him."

"I believe I shall," said the man. "I do believe I shall."

At this moment the cottage door opened, and in the lamp glow that spilled across the grass, Winnie's grandmother appeared. "Winnifred? Who are you talking to out there?"

"It's a man, Granny," she called back. "He's looking for someone." ∎

✔ Enter your reading time below. Then look up your reading speed on the Words-per-Minute table on page 130.

Reading Time _____

Reading Speed _____

Enter your reading speed on the Reading Speed graph on page 131.

Comprehension

Put an X in the box next to the correct answer for each question or statement. Do not look back at the selection.

1. What time of day does this story take place?
   ☐ a. at dawn
   ☐ b. at noontime
   ☐ c. at sunset

2. Winnie was in her yard
   ☐ a. exploring.
   ☐ b. catching fireflies.
   ☐ c. looking for her father.

3. The stranger is
   ☐ a. tall and bearded.
   ☐ b. old and sad.
   ☐ c. short and narrow.

4. As a child the stranger said he also
   ☐ a. laughed loudly.
   ☐ b. collected fireflies.
   ☐ c. played with a marionette.

5. Winnie lived in a
   ☐ a. farmhouse.
   ☐ b. country inn.
   ☐ c. cottage.

6. Winnie said she and her family had lived there
   ☐ a. for a short time.
   ☐ b. forever.
   ☐ c. for 10 years.

7. Winnie thinks the stranger should talk to her
   ☐ a. grandfather.
   ☐ b. father.
   ☐ c. grandmother.

8. Who was the stranger looking for?
   ☐ a. a family
   ☐ b. Winnie's grandmother
   ☐ c. a missing brother

✎ _____ Number of correct answers
Enter this number on the Comprehension graph on page 132.

Critical Thinking

Put an X in the box next to the best answer for each question or statement. You may look back at the selection if you'd like.

1. What kind of mood or feeling does the author create in this story?
   ☐ a. mysterious
   ☐ b. funny
   ☐ c. sad

2. The best title for this selection from the book *Tuck Everlasting* is
   - ☐ a. "Winnie Catches Fireflies."
   - ☐ b. "A Stranger Comes Visiting."
   - ☐ c. "Winnie Meets a New Friend."

3. The stranger probably stopped at Winnie's gate because
   - ☐ a. she was the first person he saw.
   - ☐ b. he had an appointment.
   - ☐ c. he was tired and needed a rest.

4. Granny's actions show that she is
   - ☐ a. protective of Winnie.
   - ☐ b. upset with Winnie.
   - ☐ c. afraid of the stranger.

5. Black ribbons had hung on the door of the cottage when
   - ☐ a. the stranger came by.
   - ☐ b. it was Halloween.
   - ☐ c. Winnie's grandfather died.

6. Which of the following is a statement of opinion rather than fact?
   - ☐ a. "My grandmother was born here."
   - ☐ b. "So of course you know everyone, and everything that goes on."
   - ☐ c. A black hat dangled from one hand.

7. The author compares the stranger to
   - ☐ a. a marionette.
   - ☐ b. Winnie's grandfather.
   - ☐ c. Winnie's father.

8. Which of the following does *not* fit with the other two?
   - ☐ a. Winnie
   - ☐ b. Granny
   - ☐ c. fireflies

✎ _____ **Number of correct answers**
Enter this number on the Critical
Thinking graph on page 133.

Vocabulary

Each numbered sentence contains an underlined word or phrase from the selection. Following are three definitions. Put an ✗ in the box next to the best meaning of the word as it is used in the sentence.

1. Winnie was once again in the yard, this time <u>intent on</u> catching fireflies.
   - ☐ a. with great doubt
   - ☐ b. determined to
   - ☐ c. taking a chance

2. His suit was a <u>jaunty</u> yellow that seemed to glow a little.
   - ☐ a. dirty
   - ☐ b. spotted
   - ☐ c. bright

3. A black hat <u>dangled</u> from one hand.
   - ☐ a. hung loosely
   - ☐ b. flew
   - ☐ c. disappeared

4. "A lovely <u>entertainment</u>."
   - ☐ a. pleasant activity
   - ☐ b. learning experience
   - ☐ c. collection

5. His tall body moved <u>continuously</u>; a foot tapped, a shoulder twitched.
   - ☐ a. like a robot
   - ☐ b. slowly
   - ☐ c. without stopping

6. At the same time he had a kind of grace, like a well-handled <u>marionette</u>.
   - ☐ a. puppet
   - ☐ b. sailor
   - ☐ c. ballet dancer

7. "I don't know anybody much," said Winnie, with a <u>shrug</u>.
   - ☐ a. a firm handshake
   - ☐ b. an intelligent smile
   - ☐ c. a lift of the shoulders

8. At this moment the cottage door opened, and in the lamp <u>glow</u> that spilled across the grass, Winnie's grandmother appeared.
   - ☐ a. flashing light
   - ☐ b. soft light
   - ☐ c. flickering light

✎ _____ **Number of correct answers**
Enter this number on the Vocabulary graph on page 134.

Personal Response

Pretend that you are the stranger and Winnie's grandmother has just asked you, "Who are you and what do you want?" What would you answer?

_____

_____

_____

_____

If you were Granny, what would you say to Winnie after the stranger left?

_____

_____

_____

_____

6 | Mystery Monsters of Loch Ness

by Patricia Lauber

Do you like mysteries? Do you like stories about monsters?
If you answered yes to both questions, you're in luck. This passage
is about a large monster that lives in a lake in Scotland.
Or does it? See what you think.

In the north of Scotland, there is a long, narrow lake. Mountains rise along its sides. Between them, the big lake stretches as far as the eye can see. The water is deep and dark. This is Loch Ness—*loch* is the Scottish word for "lake."

Loch Ness is a lake with a mystery. The mystery goes back hundreds of years. It has to do with a big, strange creature that was said to live in the loch.

Local people believed in this creature. They spoke of it as "the beastie in the loch." Most of the time, they said, the beastie lived under water. But once in a while it came to the surface. Then someone might catch sight of its head or its back or tail. What was it? No one could say, for no one ever got a good look at it. They thought it must be some kind of fish, since it lived in the loch. But it did not look like any fish they knew.

Before the 1930s, few outsiders had heard of the beastie. Then a road was built along Loch Ness. Many visitors began seeing the loch and hearing about the beastie. Some believed they had caught sight of it.

One of these sightings was written up for a local newspaper. When the editor read the story, he said, "If it's that big, we'll have to call it a monster." That was how the beastie in the loch became the Loch Ness monster. From then on, many papers printed stories about the monster. They made good reading.

These stories made the monster famous. But many readers thought it was a joke. To them, a monster was a make-believe animal, something they might see in a movie. They thought the Scots had invented a monster to draw tourists to the loch.

Accounts of the Loch Ness monster also sounded like jokes. Many people thought they had seen part of it. The parts added up to a very strange creature indeed.

It was said to be 20 or 30 feet long. The body was thick in the middle, but it thinned out toward the ends. There was a long neck with a small head. Some people had seen what looked like horns or feelers—two fleshy stalks that grew out of the head. Some had seen a stiff mane or fin on the neck and shoulders.

Sometimes the back looked like an overturned boat. At other times it had one, two, or three humps. Some people saw two or four flippers. They said the monster swam by paddling with its flippers. Other people saw no flippers. They said it swam by using its powerful tail.

The monster seemed shy. It never attacked boats or people. It was easily startled by noises, such as the slam of a car door or the putt-putt of an outboard motor. Any noise caused it to disappear. Sometimes the Loch Ness monster sank silently from sight. ■

✔ Enter your reading time below. Then look up your reading speed on the Words-per-Minute table on page 130.

　Reading Time _____

　Reading Speed _____
Enter your reading speed on the Reading Speed graph on Page 131.

Comprehension

Put an **X** in the box next to the correct answer for each question or statement. Do not look back at the selection.

1. *Loch* is the Scottish word for
   - ☐ a. scary.
   - ☐ b. monster.
   - ☐ c. lake.

2. Where is Loch Ness located?
   - ☐ a. in central Scotland
   - ☐ b. in the south of Scotland
   - ☐ c. in the north of Scotland

3. The mystery of Loch Ness goes back
   - ☐ a. hundreds of years.
   - ☐ b. thousands of years.
   - ☐ c. 50 years.

4. What did the local people call the creature in the loch?
   - ☐ a. the monster
   - ☐ b. the beastie
   - ☐ c. the big fish

5. People said that the creature lived most of the time
   - ☐ a. under water.
   - ☐ b. in a cave.
   - ☐ c. under an overturned boat.

6. Who first called the creature a monster?
   - ☐ a. a visiting tourist
   - ☐ b. a local newspaper editor
   - ☐ c. the author of this selection

7. The main reason the creature became famous is
   - ☐ a. many visitors saw it.
   - ☐ b. many papers printed stories about it.
   - ☐ c. local people talked about it.

8. Some people thought the Scots invented the monster to
   - ☐ a. keep tourists away.
   - ☐ b. amuse themselves.
   - ☐ c. draw tourists to the loch.

✎ _____ Number of correct answers
Enter this number on the Comprehension graph on page 132.

Critical Thinking

Put an **X** in the box next to the best answer for each question or statement. You may look back at the selection if you'd like.

1. The author wrote this selection to
   - ☐ a. frighten you with a monster story.
   - ☐ b. inform you about a mystery.
   - ☐ c. persuade you to visit Loch Ness.

2. Which is the most accurate statement concerning the monster's appearance?
   - ☐ a. It looks like a dinosaur.
   - ☐ b. It looks like an overturned boat.
   - ☐ c. There is no agreement about what it looks like.

3. Most people probably read the newspaper stories about the Loch Ness monster because they were
   - ☐ a. worried.
   - ☐ b. afraid.
   - ☐ c. curious.

4. Based on what you've read, you can predict that probably
   - ☐ a. no monster will ever be caught.
   - ☐ b. many monsters will be caught.
   - ☐ c. people will lose interest in the monster.

5. People thought the monster was shy because
   - ☐ a. any noise caused it to disappear.
   - ☐ b. it swam away from people.
   - ☐ c. it made very soft sounds.

6. Which of the following is a statement of opinion rather than fact?
   - ☐ a. In the north of Scotland, there is a long, narrow lake.
   - ☐ b. From then on, many papers printed stories about the monster.
   - ☐ c. Accounts of the Loch Ness Monster also sounded like jokes.

7. The many descriptions people gave of the monster were
   - ☐ a. very different from each other.
   - ☐ b. somewhat similar to each other.
   - ☐ c. identical to each other.

8. Which is the best summary of this selection?
   - ☐ a. Loch Ness has become a popular place for tourists. They come to see a mysterious monster that lives in the lake.
   - ☐ b. For hundreds of years people have reported seeing a large monster in Loch Ness. Because descriptions of it vary so much, the creature remains a mystery.
   - ☐ c. Stories about a monster living in the waters of Loch Ness are considered jokes. Many people think the stories were invented to draw tourists to the lake.

✎ _____ **Number of correct answers**
Enter this number on the Critical Thinking graph on page 133.

Vocabulary

Each numbered sentence contains an underlined word or phrase from the selection. Following are three definitions. Put an **X** in the box next to the best meaning of the word as it is used in the sentence.

1. They spoke of it as "the beastie in the loch."
   - ☐ a. mystery
   - ☐ b. creature
   - ☐ c. fish

2. <u>Local</u> people believed in this creature.
   - ☐ a. silly
   - ☐ b. crazy
   - ☐ c. nearby

3. They thought the Scots had invented a monster to <u>draw</u> tourists to the loch.
   - ☐ a. frighten away
   - ☐ b. paint
   - ☐ c. attract

4. One of these <u>sightings</u> was written up for a local newspaper.
   - ☐ a. sounds
   - ☐ b. observations
   - ☐ c. reports

5. <u>Accounts</u> of the Loch Ness monster also sounded like jokes.
   - ☐ a. stories
   - ☐ b. mysteries
   - ☐ c. flippers

6. They thought the Scots had <u>invented</u> a monster.
   - ☐ a. built
   - ☐ b. discovered
   - ☐ c. made up

7. The body was thick in the middle, but it <u>thinned out</u> toward the ends.
   - ☐ a. became wider
   - ☐ b. became narrower
   - ☐ c. became thicker

8. Sometimes the back looked like an <u>overturned</u> boat.
   - ☐ a. upside-down
   - ☐ b. speeding
   - ☐ c. large

✎ _____ **Number of correct answers Enter this number on the Vocabulary graph on page 134.**

Personal Response

Imagine that while visiting Loch Ness, you actually sighted the monster reported to be living in the lake. Write the first five to eight sentences of your own article. Describe the monster and your reaction to seeing it.

_____

_____

_____

_____

_____

_____

7 | The Great Brain at the Academy

by John D. Fitzgerald

Tom, a student at a private boy's school, has a plan to mix business with education. What kind of business is he planning? Will his friends help him carry out the plan? In this passage you'll find the answers.

Monday evening at seven twenty-five Tom made his usual announcement. "You fellows are going to have to use the washroom on the second floor for the next half hour."

Then he went inside the washroom and locked the door. He climbed through the trapdoor to the attic and opened the dormer window. In a couple of minutes he saw Daniel coming down the street. Jerry had doubted Daniel would cooperate. But Tom didn't have any doubts after learning Daniel had spent two years at the academy and stood to make fifty cents besides.

Tom let down the string with the rock tied to it. He watched Daniel remove the rock and tie the string to one end of the rope. Then he hauled it up, coiled it on the floor, and returned to the washroom. He did his cleaning job and then joined his three friends on Jerry's bunk.

"Everything went according to plan," he whispered. "Tomorrow you all start earning your ten percent."

"Hold it," Phil said. "I thought I had already earned my ten percent by getting Daniel to buy the rope for you."

"You haven't even started to earn it," Tom said. "Here is the way we will work it. Two of you will go with me to the washroom at seven thirty tomorrow night. One will have to stay and clean the washroom. The other one will go up to the attic with me to help with the rope. The third can remain in the dormitory. You will each take turns doing the different things that must be done to get the candy store going."

"Count me out," Phil said to Tom's surprise. "We will all get expelled for sure if we get caught smuggling candy into the academy."

Jerry shook his head. "What a worry wart you are," he said with disgust. "We haven't even opened the candy store and already you've got us all expelled."

"I can't help it," Phil said. "This is the only Catholic academy in Utah. And if I get expelled my mother and father will never forgive me."

Tom hadn't expected this. He looked at Tony.

"What about you, Tony?" he asked.

"Haw," Tony said.

"Cut out that haw business," Tom said. "Are you in or out?"

Tony hesitated a moment. "I think Phil is right," he said.

"In that case," Tom said, "would you and Phil mind leaving us? What I have to say is for the ears of stockholders in the corporation only. And Jerry and I will pick two other fellows to become stockholders."

Phil began biting his lip. "You mean we aren't even friends anymore?" he asked.

Jerry spoke before Tom could answer.

"Who wants to be friends with a couple of nervous old worry warts?" he asked.

"Jerry is right," Tom said. "We don't want to have anything to do with a couple of fellows who are going to be worrying all the time about something that can't even happen." ∎

✔ Enter your reading time below. Then look up your reading speed on the Words-per-Minute table on page 130.

Reading Time   _____

Reading Speed   _____

Enter your reading speed on the Reading Speed graph on Page 131.

Comprehension

Put an **X** in the box next to the correct answer for each question or statement. Do not look back at the selection.

1. Who had spent two years at the academy?
   - ☐ a. Jerry
   - ☐ b. Tom
   - ☐ c. Daniel

2. What are the boys trying to smuggle into the academy?
   - ☐ a. candy
   - ☐ b. sandwiches
   - ☐ c. magazines

3. Where does Tom plan to smuggle the goods into the academy?
   - ☐ a. through a classroom window
   - ☐ b. through an attic window
   - ☐ c. through a washroom window

4. If the boys are caught smuggling, they could
   - ☐ a. be expelled.
   - ☐ b. be suspended.
   - ☐ c. lose all their money.

5. The academy is located in the state of
   - ☐ a. California.
   - ☐ b. Idaho.
   - ☐ c. Utah.

6. In that state, the academy is the only
   - ☐ a. boy's academy.
   - ☐ b. Catholic academy.
   - ☐ c. private academy.

7. Tom calls the boys who will take part in his plan
   - ☐ a. worry warts.
   - ☐ b. stockholders.
   - ☐ c. fellow smugglers.

8. Who will pick two other fellows to join the corporation?
   - ☐ a. Tom and Jerry
   - ☐ b. Tony and Phil
   - ☐ c. Daniel

✎ _____ Number of correct answers
Enter this number on the Comprehension graph on page 132.

Critical Thinking

Put an **X** in the box next to the best answer for each question or statement. You may look back at the selection if you'd like.

1. The author probably wrote this story for readers interested in
   - ☐ a. being amused and entertained.
   - ☐ b. learning what life at a private school is like.
   - ☐ c. opening a candy store.

2. The best title for this passage from the book *The Great Brain at the Academy* is
   - ☐ a. "Best Friends."
   - ☐ b. "Living Away at School."
   - ☐ c. "Opening a Candy Store."

3. Who is the leader of the group?
   - ☐ a. Jerry
   - ☐ b. Tony
   - ☐ c. Tom

4. Based on what you've read, you can predict that
   - ☐ a. Tom and Phil will remain close friends.
   - ☐ b. Tom and Phil will no longer be friends.
   - ☐ c. Jerry and Phil will become friends.

5. Tom told Tony and Phil to leave because they
   - ☐ a. wanted more than a 10 percent share.
   - ☐ b. might tell others about the plan.
   - ☐ c. were afraid to take part in his plan.

6. Which of the following is a statement of fact rather than opinion?
   - ☐ a. "This is the only Catholic Academy in Utah."
   - ☐ b. "What a worry wart you are."
   - ☐ c. "I think Phil is right."

7. Which pair of boys were most alike?
   - ☐ a. Tom and Phil
   - ☐ b. Tony and Jerry
   - ☐ c. Tom and Jerry

8. Why does Phil bite his lip when Tom says he'll find someone else to take his place in the smuggling scheme?
   - ☐ a. He thinks the plan will fail.
   - ☐ b. He's afraid their friendship is over.
   - ☐ c. He wants to be the leader of the group.

✎ _____ **Number of correct answers**
Enter this number on the Critical Thinking graph on page 133.

Vocabulary

Each numbered sentence contains an underlined word from the article. Following are three definitions. Put an **X** in the box next to the best meaning of the word as it is used in the sentence.

1. Monday evening at seven twenty-five Tom made his usual <u>announcement</u>.
   - ☐ a. plans
   - ☐ b. speech
   - ☐ c. threat

2. Then he hauled it up and <u>coiled</u> it on the floor.
   - ☐ a. threw down
   - ☐ b. rolled up
   - ☐ c. cut up

3. Jerry had doubted Daniel would <u>cooperate</u>.
   - ☐ a. return
   - ☐ b. buy candy
   - ☐ c. help

4. "We will all get <u>expelled</u> for sure if we get caught smuggling candy into the academy."
   - ☐ a. kicked out of school
   - ☐ b. given a low grade
   - ☐ c. rewarded

5. "The third can remain in the <u>dormitory</u>."
   - ☐ a. classroom
   - ☐ b. bedroom
   - ☐ c. hallway.

6. Jerry shook his head. "What a worry wart you are," he said with <u>disgust</u>.
   - ☐ a. praise
   - ☐ b. fear
   - ☐ c. dislike

7. "Are you in or out?" Tony <u>hesitated</u> a moment. "I think Phil is right," he said.
   - ☐ a. listened
   - ☐ b. stopped
   - ☐ c. looked around

8. "What I have to say is for the ears of stockholders in the <u>corporation</u> only."
   - ☐ a. school
   - ☐ b. academy
   - ☐ c. company

✎ _____ Number of correct answers
Enter this number on the Vocabulary graph on page 134.

Personal Response

In your opinion, should Phil try to remain friends with Tom? Explain why or why not.

_____

_____

_____

I know how Tony and Phil feel because

_____

_____

_____

8 | Battle of the Ballot

Can you imagine a time when women in the United States were not allowed to vote? This selection tells about the long battle women fought to gain a right that many citizens take for granted today.

Picture yourself living in 1848. Women in the United States aren't allowed to vote. They can't own property. They can't serve on juries or even go to most colleges!

Many women were upset about these things. They knew that change had to come, and soon. In 1848, about 300 women met in Seneca Falls, New York, to hold the first Women's Rights Convention.

At this meeting, the women talked about their goals. They wanted to buy property in their own names. Like men, they wanted the right to a good education. Most important, they wanted the right to vote. With the vote, they would be the political equals of men.

For many years, women had banded together to fight social problems. Many groups had spoken out against slavery. Others fought to ban alcoholic drinks or to improve education. Word spread about the brave women in Seneca Falls. Other groups joined the fight for woman suffrage.

Two women stand out as the leaders in the struggle for the right to vote. Neither lived to see the laws changed. But their hard work started the movement. These women refused to let the dream of equal rights die.

Elizabeth Cady Stanton was the mother of six children. She was an excellent writer and speaker. Her father had been a judge. As a child, Stanton saw how unfair the law was to women, and she vowed to change it.

Mrs. Stanton's best friend was Susan B. Anthony. Anthony grew up in a Quaker family. She had been active in the fight against slavery. She had strong feelings about justice.

Anthony taught school for several years. One day, she learned that a male teacher was earning $40 a month while Anthony made only $10. The pay was different only because she was a woman. Her sense of justice told her to work for women's rights.

Anthony began to organize women to try to change the law. She planned women's meetings and conventions. She gave speeches written by Stanton, who was often busy with her young children.

In 1869, Anthony and Stanton formed the National Woman Suffrage Association (NWSA). The group's goal was an amendment to the federal Constitution that gave women the right to vote. That year another group formed called the American Woman Suffrage Association (AWSA). This group did not work toward one main law for woman suffrage. Instead, the AWSA strove for a suffrage amendment to each state constitution.

Stanton, Anthony, and many other women spoke to groups of people all over the United States. They urged citizens to write to their leaders. They asked lawmakers to change the laws. They asked men as well as women to sign petitions. The important question put to the public was "If women are citizens, why can't they vote?"

While they lived, Anthony and Stanton worked tirelessly for the cause. Other courageous women continued the fight. Finally, after 71 years of struggling, the battle was won. In 1919 Congress passed the Nineteenth Amendment, giving women the right to vote. ■

✔ Enter your reading time below. Then look up your reading speed on the Words-per-Minute table on page 130.

Reading Time _____

Reading Speed _____
Enter your reading speed on the Reading Speed graph on Page 131.

Comprehension

Put an **X** in the box next to the correct answer for each question or statement. Do not look back at the selection.

1. Which event happened in Seneca Falls, New York?
   - ☐ a. The National Woman Suffrage Association (NWSA) was formed.
   - ☐ b. The first Women's Rights Convention was held.
   - ☐ c. Women were granted the right to vote.

2. Besides the right to vote, women wanted the right to
   - ☐ a. buy property in their own names.
   - ☐ b. attend school.
   - ☐ c. drive a car.

3. How many women attended the first Women's Rights Convention?
   - ☐ a. 100
   - ☐ b. 300
   - ☐ c. 500

4. Elizabeth Cady Stanton found time to fight for women's rights despite the fact that she
   - ☐ a. grew up in a Quaker family.
   - ☐ b. taught school for several years.
   - ☐ c. was the mother of six children.

5. Before working for women's rights, Susan B. Anthony had been active in the fight
   - ☐ a. against slavery.
   - ☐ b. to protect animals.
   - ☐ c. to improve education.

6. What experience did Anthony have while teaching school that helped her decide to work for women's rights?
   - ☐ a. She was paid less than a male teacher.
   - ☐ b. She was not permitted to teach the best students.
   - ☐ c. She was only allowed to teach part-time.

7. Women's battle to win the right to vote lasted for about
   - ☐ a. 30 years.
   - ☐ b. 50 years.
   - ☐ c. 70 years.

8. The Nineteenth Amendment was passed in
   - ☐ a. 1919.
   - ☐ b. 1869.
   - ☐ c. 1848.

✎ _____ Number of correct answers
Enter this number on the
Comprehension graph on page 132.

Critical Thinking

Put an **X** in the box next to the best answer for each question or statement. You may look back at the selection if you'd like.

1. The author's main purpose was to
   - ☐ a. make you aware of women's long struggle to win the right to vote.
   - ☐ b. inform you about the lives of two remarkable women.
   - ☐ c. explain why women were so upset in 1848.

2. In the first paragraph the author
   - ☐ a. gives the setting of the story.
   - ☐ b. helps you understand why women were upset in 1848.
   - ☐ c. makes you feel sorry for women who lived in 1848.

3. Which role did Anthony and Stanton play in the Woman Suffrage movement?
   - ☐ a. followers
   - ☐ b. pioneers
   - ☐ c. volunteers

4. You can conclude that women were without the right to vote for so long because
   - ☐ a. they had no interest in voting.
   - ☐ b. men were against the idea of women voting.
   - ☐ c. women didn't understand the issues being voted on.

5. Which event happened first?
   - ☐ a. Anthony and Stanton formed the National Woman Suffrage Association (NWSA).
   - ☐ b. A women's group formed the American Woman Suffrage Association (AWSA).
   - ☐ c. A Women's Rights Convention was held in Seneca Falls, New York.

6. Anthony often gave speeches that Stanton had written because
   - ☐ a. Stanton did not like to speak in public.
   - ☐ b. Anthony was a much better public speaker.
   - ☐ c. Stanton was busy raising her young children.

7. What was the goal of the American Woman Suffrage Association (AWSA)?
   - ☐ a. an amendment to the Federal Constitution
   - ☐ b. an amendment to each state constitution
   - ☐ c. a new law

8. The most important effect of gaining the right to vote was that women were
   - ☐ a. able to own property.
   - ☐ b. the political equals of men.
   - ☐ c. allowed to serve on juries.

✎ _____ **Number of correct answers**
Enter this number on the Critical Thinking graph on page 133.

Vocabulary

Each numbered sentence contains an underlined word from the selection. Following are three definitions. Put an **X** in the box next to the best meaning of the word as it is used in the sentence.

1. At this meeting, the women talked about their goals.
   - ☐ a. points scored
   - ☐ b. things desired
   - ☐ c. problems

2. For many years women had banded together to fight social problems.
   - ☐ a. spoken
   - ☐ b. promised
   - ☐ c. joined

3. Others fought to ban alcoholic drinks or to improve education.
   - ☐ a. not allow
   - ☐ b. allow
   - ☐ c. serve

4. As a child, Stanton saw how unfair the law was to women, and she vowed to change it.
   - ☐ a. promised
   - ☐ b. hoped
   - ☐ c. decided

5. Her sense of justice told her to work for women's rights.
   - ☐ a. kindness
   - ☐ b. anger
   - ☐ c. fairness

6. Anthony began to organize women to try to change the law.
   - ☐ a. order
   - ☐ b. teach
   - ☐ c. bring together

7. Instead, the ASWA strove for a suffrage amendment to each state constitution.
   - ☐ a. hoped for
   - ☐ b. tried hard
   - ☐ c. waited

8. They urged citizens to write to their leaders.
   - ☐ a. wanted
   - ☐ b. bothered
   - ☐ c. encouraged strongly

✎ _____ **Number of correct answers**
Enter this number on the Vocabulary graph on page 134.

Personal Response

Imagine that you lived in 1848. List several reasons why you believe women should have the right to vote.

_____

_____

9 | From the Mixed-Up Files of Mrs. Basil E. Frankweiler

by E. L. Konigsburg

In this passage young Claudia decides to go on a great adventure and wants someone to go with her.

Claudia had planned her speech. "I want you, Jamie, for the greatest adventure in our lives."

Jamie muttered, "Well, I wouldn't mind if you'd pick on someone else."

Claudia looked out the window and didn't answer. Jamie said, "As long as you've got me here, tell me."

Claudia still said nothing and still looked out the window. Jamie became impatient. "I said that as long as you've got me here, you may as well tell me."

Claudia remained silent. Jamie erupted, "What's the matter with you, Claude? First you bust up my card game, then you don't tell me. It's undecent."

"Break up, not bust up. Indecent, not undecent," Claudia corrected.

"Oh, baloney! You know what I mean. Now tell me," he demanded.

"I've picked you to accompany me on the greatest adventure of our mutual lives," Claudia repeated.

"You said that." He clenched his teeth. "Now tell me."

"I've decided to run away from home, and I've chosen you to accompany me."

"Why pick on me? Why not pick on Steve?" he asked.

Claudia sighed, "I don't want Steve. Steve is one of the things in my life that I'm running away from. I want you."

Despite himself, Jamie felt flattered. (Flattery is as important a machine as the lever, isn't it? Give it a proper place to rest, and it can move the world.) It moved Jamie. He stopped thinking, "Why pick on me?" and started thinking, "I am chosen." He sat up in his seat, placed his hands over his bent knee, and said out of the corner of his mouth, "O.K., Claude, when do we bust out of here? And how?"

Claudia stifled the urge to correct his grammar again. "On Wednesday. Here's the plan. Listen carefully."

Jamie squinted his eyes and said, "Make it complicated, Claude. I like complication."

Claudia laughed. "It's got to be simple to work. We'll go on Wednesday because Wednesday is music lesson day. I'm taking my violin out of its case and am packing it full of clothes. You do the same with your trumpet case. Take as much clean underwear as possible and socks and at least one other shirt with you."

"All in a trumpet case? I should have taken up the bass fiddle."

"You can use some of the room in my case. Also use your book bag. Take your transistor radio."

"Can I wear sneakers?" Jamie asked.

Claudia answered, "Of course. Wearing shoes all the time is one of the tyrannies you'll escape by coming with me."

Jamie smiled, and Claudia knew that now was the correct time to ask. She almost managed to sound casual. "And bring all your money." She cleared her throat. "By the way, how much money do you have?"

Jamie put his foot back down on the floor, looked out the window, and said, "Why do you want to know?"

"For goodness' sake, Jamie, if we're in this together, then we're together. I've got to know. How much do you have?"

"Can I trust you not to talk?" he asked. Claudia was getting mad. ■

✔ **Enter your reading time below. Then look up your reading speed on the Words-per-Minute table on page 130.**

Reading Time _____

Reading Speed _____

Enter your reading speed on the Reading Speed graph on Page 131.

Comprehension

Put an ✗ in the box next to the correct answer for each question or statement. Do not look back at the selection.

1. Claudia is planning to
   ☐ a. go on a vacation.
   ☐ b. have a party.
   ☐ c. run away from home.

2. What was Jamie doing when Claudia interrupted him?
   ☐ a. playing a card game
   ☐ b. practicing his trumpet
   ☐ c. counting his money

3. Claudia felt the need to correct Jamie's
   ☐ a. manners.
   ☐ b. spelling.
   ☐ c. grammar.

4. Who does Claudia say she does *not* want to go with her?
   ☐ a. Steve
   ☐ b. her mother
   ☐ c. her music teacher

5. How did Jamie feel about being asked to go with Claudia?
   ☐ a. annoyed
   ☐ b. flattered
   ☐ c. not interested

6. Claudia wants to pack their clothing in
   ☐ a. paper bags.
   ☐ b. instrument cases.
   ☐ c. suitcases.

7. Claudia plays the
   ☐ a. trumpet.
   ☐ b. bass fiddle.
   ☐ c. violin.

8. Jamie wants to wear
   ☐ a. sneakers.
   ☐ b. dress shoes.
   ☐ c. boots.

✎ _____ **Number of correct answers**
Enter this number on the Comprehension graph on page 132.

42

Critical Thinking

Put an **X** in the box next to the best answer for each question or statement. You may look back at the selection if you'd like.

1. The word that best describes the mood or feeling of this selection is
   ☐ a. frightening.
   ☐ b. serious.
   ☐ c. funny.

2. Who is telling the story?
   ☐ a. an outside observer
   ☐ b. Claudia
   ☐ c. Jamie

3. Based on what you've read, you can predict that
   ☐ a. Jamie will no longer be Claudia's friend.
   ☐ b. Claudia will use Jamie's money.
   ☐ c. Claudia and Jamie will not go on the adventure.

4. What did Jamie mean when he said, "I should have taken up the bass fiddle"?
   ☐ a. He didn't like the trumpet.
   ☐ b. A bass fiddle was easier to play.
   ☐ c. A bass fiddle case had more room in it.

5. Jamie agreed to go with Claudia because he
   ☐ a. was afraid to refuse her.
   ☐ b. was flattered she asked him.
   ☐ c. had enough money to go.

6. Which of the following happened last?
   ☐ a. Claudia asked Jamie to run away with her.
   ☐ b. Claudia asked Jamie how much money he had.
   ☐ c. Jamie asked Claudia if he could wear sneakers.

7. The real reason Claudia asked Jamie to go with her is because of his
   ☐ a. great personality.
   ☐ b. musical talent.
   ☐ c. money.

8. Which of the following does *not* fit with the other two?
   ☐ a. sneaker
   ☐ b. violin
   ☐ c. trumpet

✎ _____ **Number of correct answers**
Enter this number on the Critical Thinking graph on page 133.

Vocabulary

Each numbered sentence contains an underlined word from the selection. Following are three definitions. Put an **X** in the box next to the best meaning of the word as it is used in the sentence.

1. Jamie erupted. "What's the matter with you, Claude?"
   ☐ a. burst out
   ☐ b. whispered
   ☐ c. repeated

2. "I've picked you to accompany me on the greatest adventure of our <u>mutual</u> lives," Claudia repeated.
   - [ ] a. adult
   - [ ] b. separate
   - [ ] c. shared

3. He <u>clenched</u> his teeth. "Now tell me."
   - [ ] a. cleaned
   - [ ] b. closed tightly
   - [ ] c. chewed loudly

4. "I've decided to run away from home, and I've chosen you to <u>accompany</u> me."
   - [ ] a. stay away from
   - [ ] b. come with
   - [ ] c. imagine

5. Claudia <u>stifled</u> the urge to correct his grammar again.
   - [ ] a. smothered
   - [ ] b. encouraged
   - [ ] c. continued

6. Jamie <u>squinted</u> his eyes and said, "Make it complicated, Claude. I like complication."
   - [ ] a. blinked rapidly
   - [ ] b. widened
   - [ ] c. narrowed

7. "Wearing shoes all the time is one of the <u>tyrannies</u> you'll escape by coming with me."
   - [ ] a. rules
   - [ ] b. chores
   - [ ] c. secrets

8. She almost managed to sound <u>casual</u>.
   - [ ] a. formal
   - [ ] b. wise
   - [ ] c. unconcerned

✎ _____ **Number of correct answers Enter this number on the Vocabulary graph on page 134.**

Personal Response

This statement appears in the selection: "Flattery is as important a machine as the lever, isn't it? Give it a proper place to rest, and it can move the world." What do you think this means?

_____

_____

_____

If you were Jamie, would you go with Claudia? Explain why you would or would not.

_____

_____

_____

10 | We're Having Our Say

Having Our Say: The Delany Sisters' First 100 Years is the autobiography of Sarah and Elizabeth (Bessie) Delany. The bestseller was published in 1993, when both sisters were more than 100 years old. The book was later made into a play. Bessie died in 1995 at the age of 104. Sarah was 109 years old when she died in January 1999.

The Delany sisters' father, Henry Beard Delany, was born a slave. He grew up on a Georgia plantation. Even though he was a slave, Henry Delany was taught to read and write. Later, he went to Saint Augustine's School for Negroes in Raleigh, North Carolina. There he studied to become an Episcopal priest. He went on to become the first elected black Episcopal bishop in the United States.

Their mother was Nanny James Logan Delany. She and Henry met at Saint Augustine's. Both parents worked at the school for most of their lives. They raised 10 children who all went on to finish college. Two of the Delany children became dentists. One became a doctor. Another became a lawyer and judge.

The Delany sisters were full of praise for their parents. Bessie said, "Everyone thinks their parents were special, but I *know* ours were. Our father was wise, and he was very proud of his family. We were always a loving family, very close to each other."

Sarah added that their parents gave them strong values as well as independence and a sense of pride. The sisters knew they would have to try harder than other people. When they were growing up, neither black people nor women were treated very well, and neither was expected to be successful.

In 1916, Sarah moved to New York City to study teaching. When she finished school, she applied by mail for a high school teaching job in the city schools. After three years, her name reached the top of the list of applicants. She received a letter saying that she would have to come in for an interview. Sarah knew that being black would count against her, so she skipped the appointment. She sent a letter instead, acting as if there had been a mix-up. Then she just showed up the first day of class. She became the first black teacher of domestic science in New York City.

Bessie moved to New York two years after Sarah did. She wanted to become a dentist. But New York University did not permit women to enroll in dental school. Columbia University did, so that's where Bessie went. Out of 170 students, she was the only black woman. And she was the second black woman to get a dentist's license in New York State.

Bessie and Sarah never married. When they were young, many working women chose to remain single. The sisters shared the special closeness of best friends. When asked to talk about their lives, they willingly answered questions.

Despite their closeness, the two sisters were very different. The family called Sarah "Sweet Sadie." Bessie was outspoken. She once remarked, "If Sadie is molasses, then I am vinegar. Sadie is sugar, and I'm the spice."

Sarah and Bessie thought the values they learned from their parents were good for everybody. "Be your own person, owing no one. Help others. Be proud of what you are. And struggle for the best and most education you can get." ■

✔ **Enter your reading time below. Then look up your reading speed on the Words-per-Minute table on page 130.**

Reading Time _____

Reading Speed _____
Enter your reading speed on the Reading Speed graph on Page 131.

Comprehension

Put an X in the box next to the correct answer for each question or statement. Do not look back at the selection.

1. The Delany sisters were the daughters of a
   ☐ a. dentist.
   ☐ b. teacher.
   ☐ c. former slave.

2. Their father, Henry Beard Delany, grew up in
   ☐ a. North Carolina.
   ☐ b. Georgia.
   ☐ c. New York.

3. Henry Beard Delany was the first elected black
   ☐ a. Catholic priest.
   ☐ b. Episcopal bishop.
   ☐ c. Baptist minister.

4. How many children did the parents of the Delany sisters have?
   ☐ a. 4
   ☐ b. 10
   ☐ c. 12

5. In 1916 Sarah moved to
   ☐ a. New York City.
   ☐ b. Mount Vernon, New York.
   ☐ c. Raleigh, North Carolina.

6. Bessie's desire was to become a
   ☐ a. dentist.
   ☐ b. doctor.
   ☐ c. teacher.

7. The two sisters were
   ☐ a. a little like each other.
   ☐ b. very much like each other.
   ☐ c. very different from each other.

8. The Delany sisters learned from their parents that it is important to have
   ☐ a. independence.
   ☐ b. friends.
   ☐ c. courage.

✎ _____ **Number of correct answers**
Enter this number on the Comprehension graph on page 132.

46

Critical Thinking

Put an **X** in the box next to the best answer for each question and statement. You may look back at the selection if you'd like.

1. Why do you think the author included this statement by Bessie: "If Sadie is molasses, then I am vinegar. Sadie is sugar, and I'm the spice."?
   - ☐ a. to stress how different the sisters are
   - ☐ b. to show how sweet Sadie is
   - ☐ c. to show how much alike the sisters are

2. Who is telling about the Delany sisters?
   - ☐ a. Bessie Delany
   - ☐ b. an outside observer
   - ☐ c. Henry Beard Delany

3. Why did Sarah skip her appointment to interview for a teaching job?
   - ☐ a. She didn't want them to know she was black.
   - ☐ b. She was too nervous to go.
   - ☐ c. She had a better job offer.

4. Which event happened first?
   - ☐ a. Sarah became a teacher of domestic science.
   - ☐ b. Bessie went to dental school.
   - ☐ c. Henry Delany became an Episcopal bishop.

5. Bessie went to Columbia University because New York University
   - ☐ a. was too expensive.
   - ☐ b. did not allow women into dental school.
   - ☐ c. did not allow blacks into dental school.

6. Which of the following is a statement of opinion rather than fact?
   - ☐ a. Their mother was Nanny James Logan Delany.
   - ☐ b. The sisters knew they would have to try harder than other people.
   - ☐ c. Sarah was a high school teacher.

7. Compared to Bessie, Sarah was more
   - ☐ a. quiet.
   - ☐ b. outspoken.
   - ☐ c. independent.

8. Which word best describes the Delany sisters?
   - ☐ a. lonely
   - ☐ b. dependent
   - ☐ c. independent

✎ _____ **Number of correct answers** **Enter this number on the Critical Thinking graph on page 133.**

Vocabulary

Each numbered sentence contains an underlined word from the selection. Following are three definitions. Put an **X** in the box next to the best meaning of the word as it is used in the sentence.

1. Sarah Delany was the <u>elder</u> of the two sisters.
   - ☐ a. younger
   - ☐ b. older
   - ☐ c. more respected

2. They <u>raised</u> 10 children who all went on to finish college.
   - ☐ a. brought up
   - ☐ b. lifted up
   - ☐ c. loved

3. She received a letter saying that she would have to come in for an <u>interview</u>.
   - ☐ a. a written test
   - ☐ b. a period of training
   - ☐ c. a face-to-face meeting

4. But New York University did not <u>permit</u> women to enroll in dental school.
   - ☐ a. allow
   - ☐ b. encourage
   - ☐ c. refuse

5. Bessie was <u>outspoken</u>.
   - ☐ a. not afraid to speak out
   - ☐ b. speaks out too much
   - ☐ c. speaks too loudly

6. The Delany sisters were full of <u>praise</u> for their parents.
   - ☐ a. prayers
   - ☐ b. respect
   - ☐ c. good things to say

7. When the Delany sisters were young, many working women chose to remain <u>single</u>.
   - ☐ a. brave
   - ☐ b. strong
   - ☐ c. unmarried

8. "And <u>struggle</u> for the best and most education you can get."
   - ☐ a. pay attention
   - ☐ b. work hard
   - ☐ c. think carefully

✎ _____ **Number of correct answers**
Enter this number on the Vocabulary graph on page 134.

Personal Response

Imagine you were going to interview the Delany sisters for your school newspaper. Make a list of three questions you would ask them.

_____

_____

_____

_____

✎ **Check Your Progress**
Study the graphs you completed for Lessons 1–10 and answer the How Am I Doing? questions on page 135.

11 | Mom, You're Fired!

by Nancy K. Robinson

In this passage two children try to distance themselves from their embarrassing mother.

"**I**s this the bus to Davenport Street?" Tina's mother called up to the bus driver, but he didn't seem to hear her.

Tina's mother stepped up onto the bus. She was carrying two shopping bags under one arm and Tina's little sister Angela under the other arm. Angela twisted around until she was almost hanging upside down.

"New shoes," said Angela to the man in back of her, pointing proudly to her new white shoes. "Much too esspensive," she added.

Tina and her brother Nathaniel looked at each other. Then they stepped back in line and let two ladies get in front of them. They each had their own bus fare and wanted to get as far away from their mother and little sister as possible.

They heard their mother ask in an even louder voice:

"Driver, I asked if this was the bus to Davenport Street."

"Read the sign, lady," they heard the bus driver shout.

"The sign outside is stuck," their mother said crossly.

There was no answer from the bus driver.

"Hurry up, lady," called a man at the end of the line.

Their mother wasn't in any hurry. She was giving the bus driver a lecture.

" . . . and the least you could do is tell me whether or not I'm on the right bus. It would only be common courtesy. . . ."

"Oh, no." Nathaniel grabbed Tina's arm. "Here she goes again." He pulled Tina back and let a boy carrying a large transistor radio get in front of them.

"Look lady," hollered the bus driver. "Are you getting on or off? I don't have all day."

Everyone in line was very quiet.

Tina stared hard at a crack in the sidewalk. She felt like pulling her mother off the bus and shaking her.

"Move it, lady," the man at the back of the line called again.

"It's the right bus," a lady called out. "It's a number 8. This one goes to Davenport Street."

"Thank you." Tina's mother turned around and nodded to the lady, "But I don't see why the bus driver couldn't have told me that. If I had a choice, I wouldn't even take this bus."

Nathaniel groaned. "Why can't she just get on the bus and be quiet like everyone else?"

Slowly the line of people began to move ahead.

"Nathaniel, Christina, are you there?" Now their mother was inside the bus, pounding on the window and waving at them. Tina and Nathaniel pretended not to notice.

As they were paying their fare, they saw a man get up and give their mother his seat. Tina and Nathaniel tried to squeeze to the rear of the bus, but it was too crowded to move. They were stuck right across the aisle from their mother, who had Angela on her lap.

"New shoes," said Angela to everyone who passed by.

Nathaniel grabbed onto a pole and began to read an advertisement posted above the window.

YOU TOO CAN BE A NATURAL BLONDE OR REDHEAD ■

✔ Enter your reading time below. Then look up your reading speed on the Words-per-Minute table on page 130.

Reading Time _____

Reading Speed _____

Enter your reading speed on the Reading Speed graph on Page 131.

Comprehension

Put an **X** in the box next to the correct answer for each question or statement. Do not look back at the selection.

1. Tina's mother and family were trying to get to
   - ☐ a. the shopping mall.
   - ☐ b. the back of the bus.
   - ☐ c. Davenport Street.

2. What had Tina's mother bought for Tina's little sister, Angela?
   - ☐ a. new shoes
   - ☐ b. new mittens
   - ☐ c. new glasses

3. Tina's mother asked the bus driver in a very loud voice,
   - ☐ a. "Is this the bus to Davenport Street?"
   - ☐ b. "Is this the bus to the shopping mall?"
   - ☐ c. "How much is the fare?"

4. Before getting on the bus, Tina's mother
   - ☐ a. had an argument with a lady.
   - ☐ b. gave the bus driver a lecture.
   - ☐ c. scolded Tina and Nathaniel.

5. Tina felt like
   - ☐ a. walking home.
   - ☐ b. pulling her mother off the bus and shaking her.
   - ☐ c. helping her mother get on the bus.

6. Nathaniel wished that his mother would
   - ☐ a. be quiet like everyone else.
   - ☐ b. let him sit with her.
   - ☐ c. let him sit with Tina.

7. As their mother waved to them from the window, Tina and Nathaniel
   - ☐ a. started to get on the bus.
   - ☐ b. started to walk home.
   - ☐ c. pretended not to see her.

50

8. Where did Tina and Nathaniel sit on the bus?
   ☐ a. at the back
   ☐ b. across the aisle from their mother
   ☐ c. next to the boy carrying a large radio

✎ _____ Number of correct answers
Enter this number on the
Comprehension graph on page 132.

Critical Thinking

Put an ✗ in the box next to the best answer for each question or statement. You may look back at the selection if you'd like.

1. The author wrote this story to
   ☐ a. inform you about buses.
   ☐ b. entertain you with an amusing story.
   ☐ c. persuade you that some bus drivers are rude.

2. The best title for this passage from the book *Mom, You're Fired!* is
   ☐ a. "A Shopping Trip to the City."
   ☐ b. "Embarrassed by Mother."
   ☐ c. "A Strange Bus Ride."

3. Why do you think Tina stared hard at the crack in the sidewalk?
   ☐ a. She was upset by her mother's actions.
   ☐ b. She had dropped her bus fare.
   ☐ c. She was afraid she might laugh.

4. The best word to describe Tina and Nathaniel's feelings is
   ☐ a. amused.
   ☐ b. angry.
   ☐ c. embarrassed.

5. Which event happened first?
   ☐ a. Nathaniel grabbed a pole and began to read an advertisement.
   ☐ b. A man gave Mother his seat.
   ☐ c. Mother gave the bus driver a lecture.

6. Why did Mother have to ask the driver if the bus went to Davenport Street?
   ☐ a. No one else knew.
   ☐ b. The sign on the bus was stuck.
   ☐ c. She wasn't wearing her glasses.

7. Which is the best summary?
   ☐ a. After shopping, a mother and her children ride home on a bus.
   ☐ b. A little girl shows her new shoes to everybody.
   ☐ c. A brother and sister are embarrassed when their mother causes a scene on a bus.

8. Which child probably feels differently about Mother than the other two?
   ☐ a. Angela
   ☐ b. Nathaniel
   ☐ c. Tina

✎ _____ Number of correct answers
Enter this number on the Critical Thinking graph on page 133.

Vocabulary

Each numbered sentence contains an underlined word from the selection. Following are three defintions. Put an **X** in the box next to the best meaning of the word as it is used in the sentence.

1. Angela <u>twisted</u> around until she was almost hanging upside down.
   - ☐ a. turned
   - ☐ b. flew
   - ☐ c. jumped

2. "New shoes," said Angela to the man in back of her, pointing <u>proudly</u> to her new white shoes.
   - ☐ a. straight toward
   - ☐ b. very pleased
   - ☐ c. shyly

3. They each had their own bus <u>fare</u> and wanted to get as far away from their mother and little sister as possible.
   - ☐ a. money
   - ☐ b. seat
   - ☐ c. route

4. "The sign outside is stuck," said their mother <u>crossly</u>.
   - ☐ a. angrily
   - ☐ b. excitedly
   - ☐ c. fearfully

5. She was giving the bus driver a <u>lecture</u>.
   - ☐ a. snack
   - ☐ b. talk
   - ☐ c. token

6. "Look, lady," <u>hollered</u> the bus driver.
   - ☐ a. reached out
   - ☐ b. announced
   - ☐ c. shouted

7. Nathaniel <u>groaned</u>. "Why can't she just get on the bus and be quiet like everyone else?"
   - ☐ a. moaned
   - ☐ b. greeted
   - ☐ c. laughed

8. Nathaniel grabbed onto a pole and began to read an <u>advertisement</u> posted above a window.
   - ☐ a. a public notice
   - ☐ b. a free newspaper
   - ☐ c. a book jacket

✎ _____ **Number of correct answers**
Enter this number on the Vocabulary graph on page 134.

Personal Response

How do you feel about Tina and Nathaniel trying to ignore their mother?

_____

_____

_____

12 | We Live in Mexico

by Carlos Somonte

A young boy describes growing up in a small Mexican fishing village. As you read, think about how the boy's childhood compares to your own.

My father taught me to swim when I was two years old, and I could fish by the time I was five. And now these two activities, along with exploring, are my favorite pastimes. My village, Paraiso Escondido, has water all around it. The Pacific Ocean laps onto the beach where the village is situated. There's a wide river just inland a short way, with palm trees and mangroves on its banks. So you can see that there's plenty of opportunity for me to do what I like to do most.

My village is not large enough to have a school. Only fifty families live here. So I have to travel every day, from Monday to Friday, to a nearby town for my classes. The school hours are from 8 A.M. to 2 P.M. To get there on time I have to leave the village by 7 A.M. I then get in my *cayuco*—a small wooden boat which I propel with a wooden pole—and cross the river, before walking 3 km (2 miles) to the school.

My school is an elementary school. The children here are between the ages of six and twelve. Some towns also have nursery schools for younger children, but in many rural areas these don't exist. When I'm thirteen I'll be going on to secondary school where my education will last for three years. And if I do well in my exams, I can then decide whether I should go on to high school and then to a college or perhaps to a university, or leave the educational system altogether and become a fisherman like my father. If I go on to higher education, I wouldn't finish being a student until I was twenty-four!

At school I learn Spanish—Mexico's official language—mathematics, geography, and history. But my favorite class is phys. ed. when we play football or basketball. I don't get much homework at the moment, perhaps only an hour or two to do each week, but in a year's time I expect this to increase.

When I'm on vacation, I like to get up early and explore the river in my cayuco. I always take with me a fishing line and some bait to catch catfish and some small traps called *jaiberos* for catching crabs. And with my net I catch river shrimps which Mom always likes to put in her tasty broth. I also like to climb the trees along the river banks and jump from the branches into the water.

I like living here and am looking forward to the day very soon when I can join my father fishing in the open sea from his motor boat. Then I might be able to catch a very big fish, such as a shark or barracuda! But first I need to gain some weight and grow a bit taller. Until then I'll practice fishing for catfish and other fish in the river where it's safe. ■

✔ **Enter your reading time below. Then look up your reading speed on the Words-per-Minute table on page 130.**

    Reading Time   _____

    Reading Speed   _____

Enter your reading speed on the Reading Speed graph on Page 131.

Comprehension

Put an **X** in the box next to the correct answer for each question or statement. Do not look back at the selection.

1. When he was five years old the boy learned to
   - ☐ a. swim.
   - ☐ b. fish.
   - ☐ c. explore.

2. The boy's village is situated next to the
   - ☐ a. Pacific Ocean.
   - ☐ b. Atlantic Ocean.
   - ☐ c. Andes Mountains.

3. At what time does the boy leave for school?
   - ☐ a. 7 A.M.
   - ☐ b. 8 A.M.
   - ☐ c. 2 P.M.

4. A *cayuco* is a
   - ☐ a. type of fishing pole.
   - ☐ b. trap for catching crabs.
   - ☐ c. small wooden boat.

5. The boy attends
   - ☐ a. a secondary school.
   - ☐ b. a high school.
   - ☐ c. an elementary school.

6. If the boy goes on to higher education, he wouldn't finish being a student until he was
   - ☐ a. thirteen.
   - ☐ b. eighteen.
   - ☐ c. twenty-four.

7. What language does the boy study at school?
   - ☐ a. English
   - ☐ b. Spanish
   - ☐ c. Mexican

8. What are *jaiberos*?
   - ☐ a. bait used to catch catfish
   - ☐ b. traps used to catch crabs
   - ☐ c. a kind of river shrimp

✎ _____ **Number of correct answers**
Enter this number on the Comprehension graph on page 132.

Critical Thinking

Put an **X** in the box next to the best answer for each question or statement. You may look back at the selection if you'd like.

1. In this article, who is telling about life in a Mexican village?
   - ☐ a. a young boy
   - ☐ b. a boy's father
   - ☐ c. a local fisherman

2. The boy says he needs to gain weight and grow taller because he wants to
   - ☐ a. play football and basketball.
   - ☐ b. go on to a school of higher education.
   - ☐ c. join his father fishing in the open sea.

3. Many people in the village earn a living from
   - ☐ a. entertaining tourists.
   - ☐ b. exploring the area.
   - ☐ c. fishing in the ocean.

4. Which activity did the boy learn to do first?
   - ☐ a. swimming
   - ☐ b. exploring
   - ☐ c. fishing

5. If the boy does not do well on his exams, he will not be able to
   - ☐ a. become a fisherman.
   - ☐ b. go on to high school and college.
   - ☐ c. become an explorer.

6. Which of the following is a statement of opinion rather than fact?
   - ☐ a. My village, Paraiso Escondido, has water all around it.
   - ☐ b. Some towns also have nursery schools.
   - ☐ c. Then I might be able to catch a very big fish, such as a shark.

7. You can conclude from the story that the boy is
   - ☐ a. worried about his future.
   - ☐ b. content with his life.
   - ☐ c. sad he must go away to school.

8. Which of the following does *not* fit with the other two?
   - ☐ a. basketball
   - ☐ b. swimming
   - ☐ c. fishing

✎ _____ **Number of correct answers**
Enter this number on the Critical Thinking graph on page 133.

Vocabulary

Each numbered sentence contains an underlined word from the selection. Following are three definitions. Put an **X** in the box next to the best meaning of the word as it is used in the sentence.

1. And now these two activities, along with exploring, are my favorite pastimes.
   - ☐ a. free-time fun
   - ☐ b. daily chores
   - ☐ c. childhood memories

2. The Pacific Ocean laps onto the beach where the village is situated.
   - ☐ a. folds up tightly
   - ☐ b. washes gently
   - ☐ c. sits without moving

3. So you can see there's plenty of opportunity for me to do what I like to do most.
   - ☐ a. freedom
   - ☐ b. chances
   - ☐ c. opinions

4. I then get in my *cayuco*—a small wooden boat which I <u>propel</u> with a wooden pole.
   - ☐ a. cause to move forward
   - ☐ b. make fly straight
   - ☐ c. sink

5. Some towns also have nursery schools for younger children, but in many <u>rural</u> areas these don't exist.
   - ☐ a. country
   - ☐ b. city
   - ☐ c. traffic-filled

6. At school I learn Spanish—Mexico's <u>official</u> language.
   - ☐ a. difficult to learn
   - ☐ b. no longer spoken
   - ☐ c. used by the government

7. When I'm on vacation I like to get up early and <u>explore</u> the river in my cayuco.
   - ☐ a. fish in
   - ☐ b. swim and play in
   - ☐ c. search and discover in

8. And with my net I catch river shrimps which Mom likes to put in her <u>tasty</u> broth.
   - ☐ a. good-tasting
   - ☐ b. sour
   - ☐ c. well-aged

✎ _____ **Number of correct answers Enter this number on the Vocabulary graph on page 134.**

Personal Response

What would you like about living in the Mexican village of Paraiso Escondido?

_____

_____

_____

_____

_____

What would you dislike about living there?

_____

_____

_____

_____

_____

13 | The Last Voyage of the S.S. Edmund Fitzgerald

The S.S. Edmund Fitzgerald had made many trips across the Great Lakes over the years. But this voyage would be its last.

It was a beautiful day—almost picture-perfect. The 29 crew members of the S.S. *Edmund Fitzgerald* looked forward to a pleasant journey. They had made the trip across Lake Superior many times before. Unfortunately, this time would be different.

The *Edmund Fitzgerald* was built in 1958. At the time, it was the biggest ship ever to sail on the Great Lakes. It measured 729 feet long. For 17 years, the ship had made many trips across these lakes. On November 9, 1975, it set out again, carrying thousands of tons of iron ore. The crew loaded the ore in Superior, Wisconsin. They planned to take it to Detroit, Michigan, for use in steel mills.

The ship departed at 4:30 P.M. That night, the crew received a weather update on the radio. A storm was headed their way. Captain Ernest McSorley, however, was not too concerned. The *Edmund Fitzgerald* had seen its share of storms.

Even so, McSorley took proper notice of the warning. He talked to the captain of a nearby ship, the S.S. *Arthur M. Anderson*. Just 15 miles from the *Fitzgerald*, the *Anderson* was crossing Lake Superior as well.

The two captains agreed that they should alter course. They would both steer their ships farther north, near the Canadian shore. It would be a longer route than usual, but a safer one.

By the morning of November 10, the storm had moved in. The *Fitzgerald*'s crew knew the ride ahead would be rough. November storms tended to be nasty. A bad one was called a "Witch of November." And this witch did look mean. A heavy rain was falling. The wind was gusting up to 60 miles per hour, and the crests of the waves were already 10 feet high.

By 3:00 P.M., the *Fitzgerald* was near the Canadian shore. By then, the ship had begun to list. Such listing meant that the ship was taking on water.

Meanwhile, the rain had turned to snow. The *Anderson* was still just 16 miles behind the *Fitzgerald*. But with the wind and snow, it became impossible for the two crews to see each other.

By 4:00 P.M., the wind had intensified. The gusts now reached 100 miles per hour. The waves rose 15 feet or higher.

By 6:40 P.M., the waves had reached frightening heights. Some were close to 25 feet tall. In a radio call to the *Anderson*, McSorley said it was one of the worst storms he had ever seen.

At 7:00 P.M., McSorley called the *Anderson* again to say that he was decreasing speed. That way, the Anderson could pull closer to the *Fitzgerald*. Before the call ended at 7:10 P.M., McSorley was asked if the *Fitzgerald* was still listing.

"We are holding our own," McSorley answered. No one knew it at the time, but those would be his last words to the world.

By 7:20 P.M., the *Anderson's* crew saw that the *Fitzgerald* was no longer on their radar screen. They tried to call the ship but got no answer. The *Fitzgerald* had disappeared. ■

✔ **Enter your reading time below. Then look up your reading speed on the Words-per-Minute table on page 130.**

    Reading Time _____

    Reading Speed _____
Enter your reading speed on the Reading Speed graph on Page 131.

Comprehension

Put an **X** in the box next to the correct answer for each question or statement. Do not look back at the selection.

1. The *Edmund Fitzgerald* made its last voyage in
   - ☐ a. 1958.
   - ☐ b. 1970.
   - ☐ c. 1975.

2. What was the *Edmund Fitzgerald* carrying on that last voyage?
   - ☐ a. iron ore
   - ☐ b. steel
   - ☐ c. oil

3. The *Fitzgerald* planned to deliver its cargo to
   - ☐ a. Canada.
   - ☐ b. Detroit, Michigan.
   - ☐ c. Superior, Wisconsin.

4. Storms tended to be nasty on the Great Lakes in
   - ☐ a. March.
   - ☐ b. September.
   - ☐ c. November.

5. The first sign that the *Fitzgerald* might be in trouble was when the
   - ☐ a. rain turned to snow.
   - ☐ b. ship began to list.
   - ☐ c. ship's engines stopped.

6. The crews of the *Anderson* and the *Fitzgerald* could no longer see each other because
   - ☐ a. there was too much wind and snow.
   - ☐ b. they were too far apart.
   - ☐ c. it became too dark.

7. At what time was the *Anderson's* last attempt to contact the *Fitzgerald?*
   - ☐ a. 7:20 P.M.
   - ☐ b. 4:30 P.M.
   - ☐ c. 3:00 P.M.

8. On which of the Great Lakes did the *Fitzgerald* make its last trip?
   - ☐ a. Lake Erie
   - ☐ b. Lake Michigan
   - ☐ c. Lake Superior

✎ _____ **Number of correct answers**
Enter this number on the Comprehension graph on page 132.

58

Critical Thinking

Put an **X** in the box next to the best answer for each question or statement. You may look back at the selection if you'd like.

1. The purpose of the first paragraph is to
   - ☐ a. warn you that something unusual was going to happen to the *Edmund Fitzgerald.*
   - ☐ b. let you know what the weather was like.
   - ☐ c. tell you what lake the Edmund Fitzgerald would sail across.

2. Another good title for this selection is
   - ☐ a. "An Unusual Voyage."
   - ☐ b. "Storm on Lake Superior."
   - ☐ c. "Doomed to Disaster."

3. Why wasn't Captain McSorley worried about the approaching storm?
   - ☐ a. He planned to reach port before it arrived.
   - ☐ b. His ship had survived many storms.
   - ☐ c. He planned to sail around the storm.

4. From the events in the selection, you can predict that the *Edmund Fitzgerald*
   - ☐ a. ran aground.
   - ☐ b. rode out the storm.
   - ☐ c. sank.

5. The captains of the two ships changed course because they thought it would
   - ☐ a. get them to port faster.
   - ☐ b. be a safer route.
   - ☐ c. enable them to avoid the storm.

6. Which of the following is a statement of opinion rather than fact?
   - ☐ a. It was a beautiful day—almost picture-perfect.
   - ☐ b. The *Edmund Fitzgerald* was built in 1958.
   - ☐ c. By the morning of November 10, the storm had moved in.

7. Which of the following does *not* fit with the other two?
   - ☐ a. Superior, Wisconsin
   - ☐ b. Lake Superior
   - ☐ c. Detroit, Michigan

8. The story of the *Edmund Fitzgerald* is best described as
   - ☐ a. a mystery.
   - ☐ b. a tragedy.
   - ☐ c. an adventure.

✎ _____ **Number of correct answers**
Enter this number on the Critical Thinking graph on page 133.

Vocabulary

Each numbered sentence contains an underlined word or phrase from the selection. Following are three definitions. Put an **X** in the box next to the best meaning of the word or phrase as it is used in the sentence.

1. The ship <u>departed</u> at 4:30 P.M.
   - ☐ a. arrived
   - ☐ b. left
   - ☐ c. was unloaded

2. Captain Ernest McSorley, however, was not <u>concerned</u>.
   - ☐ a. worried
   - ☐ b. careful
   - ☐ c. happy

3. The two captains agreed that they should <u>alter</u> course.
   - ☐ a. stay on
   - ☐ b. change
   - ☐ c. shorten

4. November storms tended to be <u>nasty</u>.
   - ☐ a. mild
   - ☐ b. lengthy
   - ☐ c. awful

5. The wind was gusting up to 60 miles per hour, and the <u>crests</u> of the waves were already 10 feet high.
   - ☐ a. low points
   - ☐ b. high points
   - ☐ c. spray

6. By then, the ship had begun to <u>list</u>.
   - ☐ a. tip to one side
   - ☐ b. roll over
   - ☐ c. sink

7. By 4:00 P.M. the wind had <u>intensified</u>.
   - ☐ a. become stronger
   - ☐ b. grown weaker
   - ☐ c. blown away

8. At 7:00 P.M., McSorley called the *Anderson* again to say that he was <u>decreasing speed</u>.
   - ☐ a. going faster
   - ☐ b. stopping
   - ☐ c. slowing down

✎ _____ **Number of correct answers**
Enter this number on the Vocabulary graph on page 134.

Personal Response

Write an opening paragraph for a newspaper story reporting the disappearance of the *Edmund Fitzgerald*. Be brief, using no more than three sentences.

_____

_____

_____

Thinking about this selection, I wonder why

_____

_____

_____

14 | James and the Giant Peach

by Roald Dahl

This book tells the story of a boy who meets some very odd creatures inside the pit of a giant peach. In this passage, you'll get to meet those creatures. Unfortunately, one of them seems to be quite annoyed about something.

"Lights out," said the Centipede drowsily. Nothing happened.

"Turn out the light!" he called, raising his voice.

James glanced round the room, wondering which of the others he might be talking to, but they were all asleep. The Old-Green-Grasshopper was snoring loudly through his nose. The Ladybug was making whistling noises as she breathed, and the Earthworm was coiled up like a spring at one end of his hammock, wheezing and blowing through his open mouth. As for Miss Spider, she had made a lovely web for herself across one corner of the room, and James could see her crouching right in the very center of it, mumbling softly in her dreams.

"I said turn out the light!" shouted the Centipede angrily.

"Are you talking to me?" James asked him.

"Of course I'm not talking to you," the Centipede answered. "That crazy Glow-worm has gone to sleep with her light on!"

For the first time since entering the room, James glanced up at the ceiling—and there he saw a most extraordinary sight. Something that looked like a gigantic fly without wings was standing upside down upon its six legs in the middle of the ceiling, and the tail end of this creature seemed to be literally on fire. A brilliant greenish light as bright as the brightest electric bulb was shining out of its tail and lighting up the whole room.

"Is *that* a Glow-worm?" asked James, staring at the light. "It doesn't look like a worm of any sort to me."

"Of course it's a Glow-worm," the Centipede answered. "At least that's what *she* calls herself. Although actually you are quite right. She isn't really a worm at all. Glow-worms are never worms. They are simply lady fireflies without wings. Wake up, you lazy beast!"

But the Glow-worm didn't stir, so the Centipede reached out of his hammock and picked up one of his boots from the floor. "Put out that wretched light!" he shouted, hurling the boot up at the ceiling.

The Glow-worm slowly opened one eye and stared at the Centipede. "There is no need to be rude," she said coldly. "All in good time."

"Come on!" shouted the Centipede. "Or I'll put it out for you!"

"Oh, hello, James!" the Glow-worm said, looking down and giving James a little wave and a smile. "I didn't see you come in. Welcome my dear boy, welcome—and good night!"

Then *click*—and out went the light.

James Henry Trotter lay there in the darkness with his eyes wide open, listening to the strange sleeping noises that the "creatures" were making all around him, and wondering what on earth was going to happen to him in the morning. Already, he was beginning to like his new friends very much. They were not nearly as terrible as they looked. In fact, they weren't really terrible at all. They seemed extremely kind and helpful in spite of all the shouting and arguing that went on between them.

"Good night," he whispered. ∎

✔ Enter your reading time below. Then look up your reading speed on the Words-per-Minute table on page 130.

Reading Time _____

Reading Speed _____

Enter your reading speed on the Reading Speed graph on Page 131.

Comprehension

Put an **X** in the box next to the correct answer for each question or statement. Do not look back at the selection.

1. When the centipede first asked that the light be turned off,
   - ☐ a. no one moved.
   - ☐ b. everyone jumped.
   - ☐ c. James turned off the light.

2. Who was making the whistling sound?
   - ☐ a. the Firefly
   - ☐ b. the Ladybug
   - ☐ c. the Old-Green-Grasshopper

3. James saw the Glow-worm on the
   - ☐ a. ceiling.
   - ☐ b. wall.
   - ☐ c. window.

4. The greenish light was shining out of the Glow-worm's
   - ☐ a. head.
   - ☐ b. legs.
   - ☐ c. tail.

5. The Glow-worm is really a
   - ☐ a. large earthworm.
   - ☐ b. grasshopper without legs.
   - ☐ c. lady firefly without wings.

6. Who explains to James what a Glow-worm is?
   - ☐ a. the Glow-worm
   - ☐ b. the Centipede
   - ☐ c. the Earthworm

7. James lies awake because he is
   - ☐ a. afraid of the insects.
   - ☐ b. very cold.
   - ☐ c. wondering what will happen to him.

8. James thinks that the insects are
   - ☐ a. kind and helpful.
   - ☐ b. quiet and shy.
   - ☐ c. mean and unfriendly.

✎ _____ Number of correct answers
Enter this number on the Comprehension graph on page 132.

Critical Thinking

Put an **X** in the box next to the best answer for each question or statement. You may look back at the selection if you'd like.

1. The author probably wrote this story for readers interested in
   - ☐ a. fanciful stories.
   - ☐ b. learning about insects.
   - ☐ c. realistic stories.

2. The best title for this passage from the book *James and the Giant Peach* is
   - ☐ a. "James Meets a New Friend."
   - ☐ b. "James Has an Extraordinary Experience."
   - ☐ c. "James Has Trouble Sleeping."

3. The story takes place during
   - ☐ a. the daytime.
   - ☐ b. the nightime.
   - ☐ c. dinnertime.

4. Which of the following happened first?
   - ☐ a. The Centipede hurled his boot at the ceiling.
   - ☐ b. James wondered what was going to happen to him.
   - ☐ c. The Glow-worm went to sleep with her light on.

5. The Centipede was annoyed because of
   - ☐ a. the Glow-worm's light.
   - ☐ b. Old-Green-Grasshopper's snoring.
   - ☐ c. James's talking.

6. James has
   - ☐ a. known all the insects for a long time.
   - ☐ b. known the Glow-worm for the longest time.
   - ☐ c. just recently met these insects.

7. The Earthworm is compared to a
   - ☐ a. bright electric bulb.
   - ☐ b. coiled up spring.
   - ☐ c. gigantic fly without wings.

8. Which of the following does not fit with the other two?
   - ☐ a. lady firefly
   - ☐ b. an earthworm
   - ☐ c. a glowworm.

✎ _____ **Number of correct answers**
Enter this number on the Critical Thinking graph on page 133.

Vocabulary

Each numbered sentence contains an underlined word or phrase from the selection. Following are three definitions. Put an **X** in the box next to the best meaning of the word as it is used in the sentence.

1. "Lights out," said the Centipede <u>drowsily</u>.
   - ☐ a. cheerfully
   - ☐ b. sleepily
   - ☐ c. suddenly

2. The Earthworm was <u>coiled up</u> like a spring.
   - ☐ a. wound up
   - ☐ b. walking around
   - ☐ c. sleeping sideways

3. James could see her crouching right in the very center of it, <u>mumbling</u> softly in her dreams.
   - ☐ a. speaking unclearly
   - ☐ b. rocking gently
   - ☐ c. sleeping soundly

4. James glanced up at the ceiling—and there he saw a most <u>extraordinary</u> sight.
   - ☐ a. amazing
   - ☐ b. uninteresting
   - ☐ c. horrible

5. But the Glow-worm didn't <u>stir</u>, so the Centipede reached out of his hammock and picked up one of his boots.
   - ☐ a. snore
   - ☐ b. sleep
   - ☐ c. move

6. "Put out that wretched light!" he shouted, <u>hurling</u> the boot up at the ceiling.
   - ☐ a. throwing
   - ☐ b. removing
   - ☐ c. rolling

7. "There is no need to be <u>rude</u>," she said coldly.
   - ☐ a. sick
   - ☐ b. unpleasant
   - ☐ c. serious

8. Already he was beginning to like his new friends very much. They were not nearly as <u>terrible</u> as they looked.
   - ☐ a. awful
   - ☐ b. beautiful
   - ☐ c. grumpy

✎ _____ Number of correct answers
Enter this number on the Vocabulary graph on page 134.

Personal Response

Imagine that the Centipede and the Glow-worm are real people. How would you describe the kind of person each is?

_____

_____

_____

If you were an insect, which kind would you rather be—a spider, a grasshopper, or a glowworm? Explain your choice.

_____

_____

_____

15 | Little House in the Big Woods

by Laura Ingalls Wilder

This book tells the story of a pioneer family who lived in a log cabin deep in the woods, miles from any other people. What was the family's life like? The following passage from the book will give you a good idea.

Once upon a time, many years ago, a little girl lived in the Big Woods of Wisconsin, in a little gray house made of logs.

The great, dark trees of the Big Woods stood all around the house, and beyond them were other trees and beyond them were more trees. As far as a man could go to the north in a day, or a week, or a whole month, there was nothing but woods. There were no houses. There were no roads. There were no people. There were only trees and the wild animals who had their homes among them.

Wolves lived in the Big Woods, and bears, and huge wild cats. Muskrats and mink and otter lived by the streams. Foxes had dens in the hills and deer roamed everywhere.

To the east of the little log house, and to the west, there were miles upon miles of trees, and only a few little log houses scattered far apart in the edge of the Big Woods.

So far as the little girl could see, there was only the one little house where she lived with her Father and Mother, her sister Mary, and baby sister Carrie. A wagon track ran before the house, turning and twisting out of sight in the woods where the wild animals lived, but the little girl did not know where it went, nor what might be at the end of it.

The little girl was named Laura and she called her father, Pa, and her mother, Ma. In those days and in that place, children did not say Father and Mother, nor Mamma and Papa, as they do now.

At night, when Laura lay awake in the trundle bed, she listened and could not hear anything at all but the sound of the trees whispering together. Sometimes, far away in the night, a wolf howled. Then he came nearer, and howled again.

It was a scary sound. Laura knew that wolves would eat little girls. But she was safe inside the solid log walls. Her father's gun hung over the door and good old Jack, the brindle bulldog, lay on guard before it. Her father would say,

"Go to sleep, Laura. Jack won't let the wolves in." So Laura snuggled under the covers of the trundle bed, close beside Mary, and went to sleep.

One night her father picked her up out of bed and carried her to the window so that she might see the wolves. There were two of them sitting in front of the house. They looked like shaggy dogs. They pointed their noses at the big, bright moon, and howled.

Jack paced up and down before the door, growling. The hair stood up along his back and he showed his sharp, fierce teeth to the wolves. They howled, but they could not get in.

The house was a comfortable house. Upstairs there was a large attic, pleasant to play in when the rain drummed on the roof. ■

✔ Enter your reading time below. Then look up your reading speed on the Words-per-Minute table on page 130.

Reading Time _____

Reading Speed _____

Enter your reading speed on the Reading Speed graph on Page 131.

Comprehension

Put an **X** in the box next to the correct answer for each question or statement. Do not look back at the selection.

1. The little log house was surrounded on all sides by
   - ☐ a. hills.
   - ☐ b. trees.
   - ☐ c. roads.

2. On the edge of the Big Woods, there were
   - ☐ a. a few little log houses.
   - ☐ b. some small towns.
   - ☐ c. several wagon trails.

3. Carrie is Laura's
   - ☐ a. younger sister.
   - ☐ b. older sister.
   - ☐ c. mother.

4. At night, Laura was frightened by the
   - ☐ a. roaring of a bear.
   - ☐ b. barking of dogs.
   - ☐ c. howling of wolves.

5. Laura slept on a
   - ☐ a. small cot.
   - ☐ b. trundle bed.
   - ☐ c. floor mat.

6. Who was Jack?
   - ☐ a. Laura's brother
   - ☐ b. a neighbor boy
   - ☐ c. the family dog

7. What did Laura see outside when her father carried her to the window?
   - ☐ a. two shaggy dogs
   - ☐ b. two wagon tracks
   - ☐ c. two wolves

8. How did the howling noises outside affect Jack?
   - ☐ a. They made him growl.
   - ☐ b. They frightened him.
   - ☐ c. They didn't affect him at all.

✎ _____ Number of correct answers
Enter this number on the Comprehension graph on page 132.

Critical Thinking

Put an **X** in the box next to the best answer for each question or statement. You may look back at the selection if you'd like.

1. What kind of mood or feeling does the author create in this story?
   - ☐ a. fearful
   - ☐ b. funny
   - ☐ c. lonely

2. What is this selection mainly about?
   - ☐ a. Laura's home in the woods of Wisconsin
   - ☐ b. how the wolves were a danger to Laura and her family
   - ☐ c. Laura's Ma and Pa

3. Which word best describes how Laura's father made her feel?
   - ☐ a. safe
   - ☐ b. proud
   - ☐ c. lonely

4. After learning about the wolves outside, you can predict that probably Laura's
   - ☐ a. family will move soon because it's too dangerous to stay.
   - ☐ b. family will not move away soon, but will be very careful about the wolves.
   - ☐ c. father will shoot all the wolves with his gun.

5. What caused Jack to pace up and down before the door, growling?
   - ☐ a. He wanted to go outside.
   - ☐ b. He heard the wolves howling.
   - ☐ c. He wanted to be fed.

6. Which of the following is a statement of opinion rather than fact?
   - ☐ a. Wolves lived in the Big Woods, and bears, and huge wild cats.
   - ☐ b. The little girl was named Laura.
   - ☐ c. The house was a comfortable house.

7. The author compares the wolves to
   - ☐ a. huge wild cats.
   - ☐ b. shaggy dogs.
   - ☐ c. large foxes.

8. Which of the following does *not* fit with the other two?
   - ☐ a. Jack
   - ☐ b. Mary
   - ☐ c. Carrie

✎ _____ **Number of correct answers**
Enter this number on the Critical Thinking graph on page 133.

Vocabulary

Each numbered sentence contains an underlined word from the selection. Following are three definitions. Put an **X** in the box next to the best meaning of the word as it is used in the sentence.

1. Foxes had dens in the hills and deer <u>roamed</u> everywhere.
   - ☐ a. drank water
   - ☐ b. wandered
   - ☐ c. slept

2. <u>Muskrats</u> and mink and otter lived by the streams.
   - ☐ a. kinds of water animals
   - ☐ b. kinds of water plants
   - ☐ c. people who study animals

3. A wagon <u>track</u> ran before the house, turning and twisting out of sight.
   - ☐ a. wheel marks
   - ☐ b. sound of wheels
   - ☐ c. pieces of broken wheels

4. Good, old Jack, the <u>brindle</u> bulldog, lay on guard.
   - ☐ a. jumping
   - ☐ b. mean
   - ☐ c. gray and tan

5. Laura <u>snuggled</u> under the covers of the trundle bed, close beside Mary, and went to sleep.
   - ☐ a. struggled
   - ☐ b. cuddled
   - ☐ c. shivered

6. They looked like <u>shaggy</u> dogs.
   - ☐ a. with low growls
   - ☐ b. with loud howls
   - ☐ c. with thick, rough hair

7. He showed his sharp, <u>fierce</u> teeth to the wolves.
   - ☐ a. wild
   - ☐ b. dull
   - ☐ c. friendly

8. Upstairs there was a large attic, warm and pleasant to play in when the rain <u>drummed</u> on the roof.
   - ☐ a. beat
   - ☐ b. dripped
   - ☐ c. steamed

✎ _____ **Number of correct answers**
Enter this number on the Vocabulary graph on page 134.

Personal Response

Pretend that you, like Laura, lived many years ago in a log cabin deep in the woods. Other than your family, no other people live nearby. What would you like about your life there?

_____

_____

_____

_____

What would you dislike about your life there?

_____

_____

_____

_____

_____

16 Racing on the Wind

by Edward and Ruth S. Radlauer

For centuries people have wanted to soar through the sky like birds.
The sport of hang gliding brings us closest to fulfilling that wish.
This passage describes how it's possible to soar with the birds.

When the wind blows, many things go. The things and the people in them may go up, down, around, or whatever way the wind goes. They may go over water, on the water, over land, or on land.

History is filled with stories of people who used wind and air for fun and travel. One story that goes back about 3,000 years into history tells of two Greek men who escaped from prison by using wings made of feathers and wax. The story says the wax wings melted when one man flew too near the sun. His feathers fell off and he crashed into the sea.

If those Greeks had used *hang glide* or *self-soaring* wings for their prison escape, there wouldn't have been any wax for the sun to melt. Of course, no one believes they got near the sun, anyway.

For self-soaring or hang gliding there should be wind, plenty of it. A wind of 20 miles per hour or more is good for flying. Before flying, a rider sets up his kite at the top of a hill. The kite must be unfolded and set up facing into the wind. If the front or point isn't facing into the wind, the kite may go flying without the rider.

Hang glide kites are made of tightly woven cloth, lightweight metal rods, and strong wires. The cloth is so tightly woven that it's almost airtight. The rods and wires should be made of very strong material. If something should break during a flight—well, remember the Greeks.

People have always wanted to fly, and people have always wanted to add beauty to their lives. Beauty can come from colors, shapes, and forms. Self-soaring people add beauty to their kites with colors and decorations.

Quite often a person may have a kite custom-made by a professional kite builder. The kite builder can let the buyer pick the cloth for color and decoration. But when it comes to the shape, the professional builder doesn't let the buyer have much say. A kite has to be built to fly. That's why the shape is important. People who build their own kites can decorate them any way they like, but if the shape isn't right, they wouldn't do much flying.

After being strapped in, a hang glide kite flier is ready to go. The flight starts with a downhill run into the wind. The wind catches the kite and gives the rider the lift needed to fly. For the first part of the ride, the rider tries for speed and altitude. Without these, a flight may be over before it even starts.

As soon as the kite gains speed and altitude, a flier can start to control the direction of flight. For a right turn, the rider leans to the right and moves the steering bar to the left. This tips the kite to the right and it makes a turn. For a left turn, the rider leans left. ∎

✔ Enter your reading time below. Then look up your reading speed on the Words-per-Minute table on page 130.

    Reading Time   _____

    Reading Speed   _____
Enter your reading speed on the Reading Speed graph on Page 131.

Comprehension

Put an **X** in the box next to the correct answer for each question or statement. Do not look back at the selection.

1. One story tells of two Greek men who escaped from prison using wings made of
   - ☐ a. silk cloth and thread.
   - ☐ b. feathers and wax.
   - ☐ c. strong paper and wires.

2. The story of those two Greek men goes back into history about
   - ☐ a. 3,000 years.
   - ☐ b. 1,000 years.
   - ☐ c. 500 years.

3. How strong a wind is needed for good hang gliding?
   - ☐ a. 10 miles per hour
   - ☐ b. 20 miles per hour
   - ☐ c. 35 miles per hour

4. A rider should set up his kite
   - ☐ a. on a flat, open field.
   - ☐ b. on a mountain top.
   - ☐ c. at the top of a hill.

5. The kite must be set up with its front
   - ☐ a. facing away from the wind.
   - ☐ b. pointed sideways to the wind.
   - ☐ c. facing into the wind.

6. Hang glide kites are made of
   - ☐ a. tightly woven cloth and metal rods.
   - ☐ b. plastic sheets and wooden braces.
   - ☐ c. lightweight aluminum and wires.

7. Who decides what shape a kite will be?
   - ☐ a. the kite builder
   - ☐ b. the kite buyer
   - ☐ c. the kite flier

8. As soon as the kite begins traveling high enough and fast enough, the hang glide flier can
   - ☐ a. sit back and relax.
   - ☐ b. start to control the direction of flight.
   - ☐ c. fly without any wind.

✎ _____ Number of correct answers
Enter this number on the Comprehension graph on page 132.

Critical Thinking

Put an X in the box next to the best answer for each question or statement. You may look back at the selection if you'd like.

1. The author's main purpose in writing this selection was to
   - ☐ a. inform you of the history of hang gliding.
   - ☐ b. instruct you how to build a hang glide kite.
   - ☐ c. inform you about the sport of hang gliding.

2. Which of the following seems to be most important in building a hang glide kite?
   - ☐ a. the color of the kite
   - ☐ b. the kind of materials used
   - ☐ c. the shape of the kite

3. The fact that history is filled with stories of people who used wind and air for fun and travel shows that people have
   - ☐ a. always wanted to fly.
   - ☐ b. feared flying since the time of the ancient Greeks.
   - ☐ c. wanted to fly only since the 20th century.

4. After being strapped in, a hang glide flier begins the flight by
   - ☐ a. running downhill into the wind.
   - ☐ b. gaining speed and altitude.
   - ☐ c. controlling the direction of flight.

5. What could happen if a hang glide kite isn't facing into the wind when it is set up?
   - ☐ a. It will not lift off the ground.
   - ☐ b. It may blow away without the rider.
   - ☐ c. It could be torn apart by the wind.

6. You could say that people who fly hang gliders tend to be
   - ☐ a. shy.
   - ☐ b. restless.
   - ☐ c. daring.

7. In one way, the two Greek men who escaped from prison were like
   - ☐ a. kites.
   - ☐ b. birds.
   - ☐ c. fish.

8. Based on the selection, which of the following does *not* fit with the other two?
   - ☐ a. tightly woven cloth
   - ☐ b. feathers
   - ☐ c. lightweight metal rods

✎ _____ **Number of correct answers**
Enter this number on the Critical Thinking graph on page 133.

Vocabulary

Each numbered sentence contains an underlined word from the selection. Following are three definitions. Put an X in the box next to the best meaning of the word as it is used in the sentence.

1. For self-soaring or hang gliding there should be wind, plenty of it.
   - ☐ a. a way of flying without power
   - ☐ b. something out of the ordinary
   - ☐ c. facing into the wind

2. A wind of 20 miles <u>per</u> hour is good for flying.
   - ☐ a. for every
   - ☐ b. through
   - ☐ c. by

3. Hang glide kites are made of tightly <u>woven</u> cloth, lightweight metal rods, and strong wires.
   - ☐ a. stretched on all sides
   - ☐ b. shaped into a triangle
   - ☐ c. made by weaving

4. The cloth is so tightly woven that it's almost <u>airtight</u>.
   - ☐ a. waterproof
   - ☐ b. without holes
   - ☐ c. lightweight

5. A person may have a kite <u>custom-made</u> by a professional kite builder.
   - ☐ a. test-flown
   - ☐ b. specially made
   - ☐ c. decorated by hand

6. But when it comes to the shape, the <u>professional</u> builder doesn't let the buyer have much to say.
   - ☐ a. in training
   - ☐ b. working to earn a ilving
   - ☐ c. having a hobby

7. For the first part of the ride, the rider tries for speed and <u>altitude</u>.
   - ☐ a. strength
   - ☐ b. distance
   - ☐ c. height

8. As soon as the kite gains speed and altitude, a flier can <u>control</u> the direction of flight.
   - ☐ a. guide
   - ☐ b. stop
   - ☐ c. push

✎ _____ **Number of correct answers**
Enter this number on the Vocabulary graph on page 134.

Personal Response

Do you think authors should have firsthand experience with the things they write about? Explain why or why not.

_____

_____

_____

A question I would like the authors to answer about hang gliding is

_____

_____

_____

17 | Henry Reed's Journey

by Keith Robertson

Henry Harris Reed keeps a journal in which he records his thoughts and feelings about his daily life. You get a chance to read a part of the journal in this passage.

My name is Henry Harris Reed and this is my journal. It is my private property and in case it gets lost, please return it to me in care of my uncle, Mr. J. Alfred Harris, RD 1, Grover's Corner, Princeton, N.J. I'll send you whatever you spend in postage. It's important that I get it back as I am going to make it into a book and publish it.

I guess I'd better explain how I happen to be flying to San Francisco. My father is in the diplomatic service. Last summer we were living in Naples, and I flew to the United States and spent the summer with my Uncle Al and Aunt Mabel in Grover's Corner, New Jersey. I had a lot of fun, and I guess my aunt and uncle didn't mind having me too much, because they invited me back again this summer. This time, however, I am not crossing the Atlantic Ocean. About six months ago my father was transferred to Manila, and so I am flying across the Pacific and will arrive in San Francisco.

Last year I kept a journal of what I did and used it as a report when school opened. I got an "A" on it. Miss Prescott, my English teacher, said it was very good, although she did complain about the pages being sort of grimy. She says anyone who keeps a journal should always wash his hands before writing in it just as he should before meals. That's silly. Can you imagine Robinson Crusoe going down to the stream and washing his hands every time he wrote in his journal? He would have been caught by the cannibals long before he finished his book. Probably what upset Miss Prescott was the angleworm that got pressed between pages 42 and 43. I remember using a worm as a marker, but I wouldn't have closed the notebook on it. I wonder if Midge could have done that? That's the sort of trick she'd think was hilarious.

Midge Glass was my partner in a research business in Grover's Corner last summer. She was the only person under forty living there, so I didn't have much choice. She turned out to be a good sport and very smart, even if she is a girl. We got to be very good friends. Midge doesn't giggle, and giggling is the main thing wrong with most girls.

Mr. Glass is a research chemist, and he is attending a convention in San Francisco. Midge and Mrs. Glass are with him, and they are all going to drive back to New Jersey. The trip is their vacation. Since I was due to arrive in San Francisco at the same time they planned to be there, I was invited to drive back with them. That was a lucky break for me, and I am looking forward to the trip. I've been all over Europe and part of Asia, but I haven't seen much of the United States. ∎

✔ Enter your reading time below. Then look up your reading speed on the Words-per-Minute table on page 130.

Reading Time _____

Reading Speed _____

Enter your reading speed on the Reading Speed graph on Page 131.

Comprehension

Put an **X** in the box next to the correct answer for each question or statement. Do not look back at the selection.

1. If his journal gets lost, Henry would like it returned to
   □ a. Rhode Island.
   □ b. New Jersey.
   □ c. San Francisco.

2. While he is writing his journal entry, Henry is
   □ a. on a diplomatic mission.
   □ b. flying to San Francisco.
   □ c. crossing the Atlantic Ocean.

3. Where did Henry live last summer?
   □ a. Grover's Corner
   □ b. Manila
   □ c. Naples

4. Henry's English teacher is
   □ a. Mr. Glass.
   □ b. Mr. J. Alfred Harris.
   □ c. Miss Prescott.

5. Who is Midge?
   □ a. Henry's younger sister
   □ b. Henry's good friend
   □ c. a research chemist

6. Mr. Glass is in San Francisco because he
   □ a. is attending a convention.
   □ b. lives there.
   □ c. is on vacation.

7. Mr. Glass is
   □ a. a research chemist.
   □ b. in the diplomatic service.
   □ c. a travel agent.

8. Henry is glad to be traveling in the Glasses' car because he will be able to
   □ a. visit the Atlantic Ocean again.
   □ b. see some of the United States.
   □ c. enjoy Mr. Glass's company.

✎ _____ Number of correct answers
Enter this number on the Comprehension graph on page 132.

Critical Thinking

Put an **X** in the box next to the best answer for each question or statement. You may look back at the selection if you'd like.

1. Who is telling this story?
   □ a. Midge Glass
   □ b. Mr. J. Alfred Harris
   □ c. Henry Harris Reed

2. The best title for this selection from the book *Henry Reed's Journey* is
   □ a. "Henry Reed Sees the United States."
   □ b. "A Visit to Grover's Corner, N.J."
   □ c. "Henry Reed's Journal."

74

3. You can conclude that Grover's Corner
   - [ ] a. has few children.
   - [ ] b. attracts many tourists.
   - [ ] c. is close to San Francisco.

4. Based on what you've read, you can predict that Henry's family will probably
   - [ ] a. settle down and live in Grover's Corner.
   - [ ] b. settle down and live in San Francisco.
   - [ ] c. continue to move often.

5. Henry's journal is very important to him because he
   - [ ] a. needs it for a school report.
   - [ ] b. is going to make it into a book and publish it.
   - [ ] c. wants to give it to Midge Glass.

6. Which of the following is a statement of opinion rather than fact?
   - [ ] a. Last summer we were living in Naples.
   - [ ] b. I've been all over Europe and part of Asia.
   - [ ] c. Anyone who keeps a journal should always wash his hands before writing in it.

7. In what way has Henry's life been different from Midge's?
   - [ ] a. Henry once had a research business.
   - [ ] b. Henry has traveled all over the world.
   - [ ] c. Henry has lived in Grover's Corner, N.J.

8. Which of the following does *not* fit with the other two?
   - [ ] a. Naples
   - [ ] b. Manila
   - [ ] c. Grover's Corner

✎ _____ **Number of correct answers**
Enter this number on the Critical Thinking graph on page 133.

Vocabulary

Each numbered sentence contains an underlined word from the selection. Following are three definitions. Put an **X** in the box next to the best meaning of the word as it is used in the sentence.

1. It is my <u>private</u> property and in case it gets lost, please return it to me.
   - [ ] a. legal
   - [ ] b. borrowed
   - [ ] c. personal

2. I'm going to make it into a book and <u>publish</u> it.
   - [ ] a. print
   - [ ] b. sign
   - [ ] c. read

3. I guess I'd better <u>explain</u> how I happen to be flying to San Francisco.
   - [ ] a. ask
   - [ ] b. tell
   - [ ] c. wonder

4. About six months ago my father was <u>transferred</u> to Manila, and so I am flying across the Pacific and will arrive in San Francisco.
   - ☐ a. introduced
   - ☐ b. moved
   - ☐ c. visited

5. She did complain about the pages being sort of <u>grimy</u>.
   - ☐ a. complicated
   - ☐ b. rude
   - ☐ c. dirty

6. That's the sort of trick she'd think was <u>hilarious</u>.
   - ☐ a. sincere
   - ☐ b. sad
   - ☐ c. funny

7. Midge Glass was my <u>partner</u> in a research business in Grover's Corner last summer.
   - ☐ a. co-worker
   - ☐ b. enemy
   - ☐ c. boss

8. I was <u>due</u> to arrive in San Francisco at the same time they planned to be there.
   - ☐ a. about
   - ☐ b. expected
   - ☐ c. delayed

✎ _____ **Number of correct answers Enter this number on the Vocabulary graph on page 134.**

Personal Response

Because of his father's job, Henry Reed has lived in different foreign countries and has had to move often. Explain why you would or would not like the kind of life Henry has.

_____

_____

_____

Henry Reed says that he hasn't seen much of the United States. Write Henry a note describing a place in the United States that he should see and explain why.

_____

_____

_____

18 | The Boston Marathon

A running event that began many years ago, with few runners and few people to watch it, has grown into one of the world's most famous sporting events. This selection tells how the Boston Marathon came to be.

Each year for over 100 years, runners have gathered outside of Boston, Massachusetts. They toe the starting line. They hear the starting gun, jump into motion, and race to the finish line. It is not an easy race. The finish line is in downtown Boston, more than 26 miles away.

This yearly event is known as the Boston Marathon. Runners from around the world compete in the race. The Boston Marathon has become a huge sporting event. Many runners feel that it is the most prestigious race of the year. To them, the race is second only to the Olympics.

The first "marathon" took place in ancient Greece. In 490 B.C., the Greeks won a battle at a town called Marathon. A Greek soldier carried the news to Athens. He ran all the way—about 25 miles.

In 1896, the modern Olympics were established. The organizers chose to honor the ancient "marathon." They added a marathon race to the Olympics. The course was 25 miles long. In 1908, the distance was changed to 26 miles, 385 yards—the course length for all modern marathons.

The first Boston Marathon took place on April 19, 1897. Fifteen runners lined up in a small town near Boston. They ran 25 miles into the city. Most of the course was dirt roads. There was no prize money, and few people came to watch.

This humble event was the start of a great tradition. Today, the Boston Marathon is the oldest annual marathon. It has been called "the Super Bowl of foot racing." Nearly 40,000 men and women ran the race in 1996. About two million people lined the roads to watch. Now the roads of the course are paved. And Marathon winners earn prize money, fame, and glory.

In the early years of the Boston Marathon, running was not a popular sport. Few runners took part in the race. Most people thought the runners were odd. Why put themselves through the pain?

In the 1960s, people's views about running started to change. Doctors began to prove that running can promote good health. People soon realized that running has many perks. It is great exercise, it is free, and it requires little equipment. It can be done just about anytime, anywhere. And just about anyone can run.

More and more people began to jog and run. Suddenly, running was a popular pastime. Some people ran just a few miles a week. Others began to run 50 miles or more per week. Still others began to wonder if they too could run in a marathon. More and more people signed up to run the Boston race.

By the 1970s, thousands entered the Boston Marathon each year. They came from every state and almost every country. In fact, too many people wanted to enter the race. The course could not hold them all. So the organizers made a rule. Runners now had to qualify. They had to prove they could run the distance in a set time. ■

✔ **Enter your reading time below. Then look up your reading speed on the Words-per-Minute table on page 130.**

Reading Time _____

Reading Speed _____

Enter your reading speed on the Reading Speed graph on Page 131.

Comprehension

Put an **X** in the box next to the correct answer for each question or statement. Do not look back at the selection.

1. To many runners, the Boston Marathon is second only to the
   - ☐ a. Olympics.
   - ☐ b. New York City Marathon.
   - ☐ c. Indianapolis 500 Race.

2. Runners who compete in the race come from all around
   - ☐ a. the country.
   - ☐ b. Massachusetts.
   - ☐ c. the world.

3. Where did the first marathon take place?
   - ☐ a. Greece
   - ☐ b. Rome
   - ☐ c. Boston

4. The first Boston Marathon took place in
   - ☐ a. 490 B.C.
   - ☐ b. 1897.
   - ☐ c. 1908.

5. Runners in the first Boston Marathon ran on a course that was mostly
   - ☐ a. dirt roads.
   - ☐ b. paved roads.
   - ☐ c. downhill.

6. The Boston Marathon has been called the
   - ☐ a. "World Championship of foot racing."
   - ☐ b. "World Series of foot racing."
   - ☐ c. "Super Bowl of foot racing."

7. The number of people lining the road to watch the race has grown to about
   - ☐ a. 40,000.
   - ☐ b. 1 million.
   - ☐ c. 2 million.

8. What did people begin to think about running in the 1960s?
   - ☐ a. They believed running was too painful.
   - ☐ b. They realized running had many benefits.
   - ☐ c. They thought runners were odd.

✎ _____ **Number of correct answers**
Enter this number on the Comprehension graph on page 132.

Critical Thinking

Put an **X** in the box next to the best answer for each question or statement. You may look back at the selection if you'd like.

1. The author's main purpose in the first paragraph of the selection is to let you know that the
   - ☐ a. Boston Marathon is not an easy race.
   - ☐ b. Boston Marathon has a long tradition.
   - ☐ c. finish line of the Boston Marathon is in downtown Boston.

2. Which sentence best states the main idea of the selection?
   - ☐ a. Winners of the Boston Marathon now earn prize money, fame, and glory.
   - ☐ b. The Boston Marathon is the oldest and most important annual marathon.
   - ☐ c. Running has not always been a popular sport.

3. Why did some people think early marathon runners were odd?
   - ☐ a. The runners did not get paid.
   - ☐ b. The runners put themselves through pain.
   - ☐ c. The runners often ran in cold weather.

4. Which event happened last?
   - ☐ a. The first Boston Marathon took place.
   - ☐ b. The modern Olympics were established.
   - ☐ c. The Greeks won a battle at Marathon.

5. Why did the organizers of the Boston Marathon have to make a rule about who could enter the race?
   - ☐ a. Too many people wanted to enter the race.
   - ☐ b. They wanted more people to enter the race.
   - ☐ c. They didn't want women to enter the race.

6. Which of the following is a statement of opinion rather than fact?
   - ☐ a. Today, the Boston Marathon is the oldest annual marathon.
   - ☐ b. In 1896, the modern Olympics were established.
   - ☐ c. The Boston Marathon is the most important race of the year.

7. How does the course length of the early marathons compare with the length of modern marathons?
   - ☐ a. The early marathons were shorter in length.
   - ☐ b. The early marathons were longer in length.
   - ☐ c. The course length was the same.

8. Which of the following does *not* fit with the other two?
   - ☐ a. Marathon
   - ☐ b. Athens
   - ☐ c. Boston

✎ _____ **Number of correct answers**
Enter this number on the Critical Thinking graph on page 133.

Vocabulary

Each numbered sentence contains an underlined word from the selection. Following are three definitions. Put an **X** in the box next to the best meaning of the word as it is used in the sentence.

1. Many runners feel that it is the most <u>prestigious</u> race of the year.
   - ☐ a. difficult
   - ☐ b. crowded
   - ☐ c. important

2. In 1896, the modern Olympics were <u>established</u>.
   - ☐ a. set up
   - ☐ b. honored
   - ☐ c. discussed

3. The <u>humble</u> event was the start of a great tradition.
   - ☐ a. very old
   - ☐ b. great
   - ☐ c. not important

4. Today, the Boston Marathon is the oldest <u>annual</u> marathon.
   - ☐ a. happening every two years
   - ☐ b. happening once a year
   - ☐ c. happening in the spring

5. In the early years of the Boston Marathon, running was not a <u>popular</u> sport.
   - ☐ a. difficult
   - ☐ b. well-liked
   - ☐ c. forgotten

6. In the 1960s, people's <u>views</u> about running started to change.
   - ☐ a. opinions
   - ☐ b. worries
   - ☐ c. something seen

7. People soon realized that running has many <u>perks</u>.
   - ☐ a. benefits
   - ☐ b. friends
   - ☐ c. problems

8. So the organizers made a rule. Runners now had to <u>qualify</u> to enter.
   - ☐ a. sign up
   - ☐ b. train hard
   - ☐ c. gain the right

✎ _____ **Number of correct answers**
Enter this number on the Vocabulary graph on page 134.

Personal Response

Would you ever want to be a long-distance runner and compete in a marathon? Explain why or why not.

_____

_____

_____

_____

19 | The Good-Guy Cake

by Barbara Dillon

It's not easy being the youngest member of your family. This is especially true when your older sister yells at you and your mother is annoyed with you—for a good reason. In this passage young Martin Bennett wants his mother to be in a good mood.

"**M**artin Bennett, get out of my closet this instant!" yelled Martin's sister, Mary. "What are you doing in this room anyway?"

"I'm looking for my ball," explained Martin, backing hastily toward the door.

"Well, it's not in here," Mary said. She looked at her brother more closely. "What have you got all over your mouth?" she demanded.

"Nothing," said Martin, nervously putting his sticky hands behind his back.

"It's chocolate!" Mary screamed. "You found that Mars Bar in my sewing box. You stole my candy!"

Martin didn't stop to answer. He turned and ran.

"If I ever find you in here again, I'll kill you!" Mary shouted after him.

Martin bounded downstairs just as fast as his legs could carry him.

"Martin, look what you're doing to my new wallpaper!" cried his mother. She was standing in the hallway glaring up at him. Martin glanced in alarm at the wall next to him. It was covered with chocolatey finger marks.

Oh-oh, I'm in trouble, he thought.

"How many times have I told you to keep your hands off the wall and use the banister?" his mother wailed. "That's what it's there for."

"I'm sorry," said Martin. "I'll remember next time."

He particularly wanted his mother to be in a good mood today, because he had something very important to ask her, something he and his best friend, Charlie Miles, had just finished talking about on the telephone. As a matter of fact, he had been on his way downstairs to find her when he had been sidetracked by the interesting possibilities of Mary's empty room. Now he would have to wait awhile until his mother cooled off.

Martin went into the living room and snapped on the television. He snapped it off again, got down on his hands and knees to look for a quarter that he had lost under the couch the week before, and then, figuring he had given his mother enough time to recover, headed doggedly for the kitchen.

Mrs. Bennett was busy swabbing the floor with her sponge mop.

"Don't come in," she said sharply. "The floor is all wet."

"Can-I-go-to-the-school-fair-next-week-on-my-bike-Charlie-Miles'-mom-is-letting-him-and-I-would-be-very-careful-and-ride-over-to-the-side-of-the-road-so-I-don't-get-killed." Martin took a deep breath and looked eagerly at his mother.

"You would have to go along the Post

Road to get to the school," Mrs. Bennett said, without looking up from her mopping. "There would be too much traffic. I would worry the whole time you were gone."

"Charlie Miles' mom isn't going to worry," said Martin. "And I'm a better rider than Charlie is."

"Well, I can't help it. I would worry," said his mother, squeezing out the mop into the bucket at her side.

"I would go really slowly and not try anything crazy," Martin promised.

"No," said his mother firmly. ■

✔ Enter your reading time below. Then look up your reading speed on the Words-per-Minute table on page 130.

Reading Time _____

Reading Speed _____

Enter your reading speed on the Reading Speed graph on Page 131.

Comprehension

Put an X in the box next to the correct answer for each question or statement. Do not look back at the selection.

1. What did Martin say he was looking for in his sister's room?
   ☐ a. some candy
   ☐ b. a ball
   ☐ c. her diary

2. What had Mary hidden in her sewing box?
   ☐ a. money
   ☐ b. her diary
   ☐ c. a chocolate bar

3. Martin's mother told him to
   ☐ a. use the banister.
   ☐ b. stay out of his sister's room.
   ☐ c. wash the wallpaper.

4. Martin wanted his mother to be in a good mood because
   ☐ a. his sister was mad at him.
   ☐ b. he had something very important to ask her.
   ☐ c. he had to telephone Charlie.

5. Charlie is Martin's
   ☐ a. best friend.
   ☐ b. brother.
   ☐ c. next-door neighbor.

6. Martin looked for the lost quarter
   ☐ a. under the couch.
   ☐ b. behind the television.
   ☐ c. in the kitchen.

7. Martin asked his mother if he could
   ☐ a. play ball with Charlie.
   ☐ b. go to Charlie's house.
   ☐ c. bike to the school fair.

8. Why doesn't Martin's mother want him biking on the Post Road?
   ☐ a. It's too bumpy to travel on.
   ☐ b. It has too much traffic.
   ☐ c. It's too lonely.

✎ _____ Number of correct answers
Enter this number on the Comprehension graph on page 132.

Critical Thinking

Put an **X** in the box next to the best answer for each question or statement. You may look back at the selection if you'd like.

1. The author tells this story mainly by
   - ☐ a. retelling a personal experience.
   - ☐ b. comparing Martin's and Charlies's families.
   - ☐ c. using her imagination.

2. This selection is mainly about Martin's
   - ☐ a. efforts to bike to the school fair.
   - ☐ b. soiling of the wallpaper with chocolate.
   - ☐ c. taking his sister's candy bar.

3. The actions of Martin's mother show that she
   - ☐ a. doesn't like Martin's friend Charlie.
   - ☐ b. is concerned for Martin's safety.
   - ☐ c. is angry about Martin's carelessness.

4. Based on what happened, you can tell that Martin and his sister
   - ☐ a. get along well together.
   - ☐ b. try to ignore each other.
   - ☐ c. often fight with each other.

5. Why wouldn't Martin's mother let him come into the kitchen?
   - ☐ a. The floor was all wet.
   - ☐ b. She was still angry with him.
   - ☐ c. She was painting the walls.

6. Which of the following is a statement of fact rather than opinion?
   - ☐ a. "Charlie Miles' mom isn't going to worry."
   - ☐ b. Martin went into the living room and snapped on the television.
   - ☐ c. "And I'm a better rider than Charlie is."

7. According to what Martin has said, his mother is probably different from Charlie's mother in which way?
   - ☐ a. She has a more easy-going manner.
   - ☐ b. She is less concerned about safety.
   - ☐ c. She worries more.

8. Which event happened first?
   - ☐ a. Martin talked to Charlie on the phone.
   - ☐ b. Martin's mother washed the kitchen floor.
   - ☐ c. Martin was caught eating his sister's candy bar.

✎ _____ **Number of correct answers**
Enter this number on the Critical Thinking graph on page 133.

Vocabulary

Each numbered sentence contains an underlined word from the selection. Following are three definitions. Put an X in the box next to the best meaning of the word as it is used in the sentence.

1. "I'm looking for my ball," explained Martin, backing hastily toward the door.
   - ☐ a. clumsily
   - ☐ b. quickly
   - ☐ c. steadily

2. Martin bounded downstairs just as fast as his legs could carry him.
   - ☐ a. walked
   - ☐ b. fall
   - ☐ c. jumped

3. She was standing in the hallway glaring up at him.
   - ☐ a. staring angrily
   - ☐ b. winking slyly
   - ☐ c. smiling sweetly

4. Martin glanced in alarm at the wall next to him. It was covered with chocolatey finger marks.
   - ☐ a. excitement
   - ☐ b. fear
   - ☐ c. giggles

5. He had been on his way downstairs when he was sidetracked by the interesting possibilities of Mary's empty room.
   - ☐ a. distracted
   - ☐ b. silenced
   - ☐ c. attacked

6. Then, figuring he had given his mother enough time to recover, headed doggedly for the kitchen.
   - ☐ a. stubbornly
   - ☐ b. shyly
   - ☐ c. loudly

7. Mrs. Bennett was busy swabbing the floor with her sponge mop.
   - ☐ a. brushing
   - ☐ b. washing
   - ☐ c. painting

8. "No," said his mother firmly.
   - ☐ a. sternly
   - ☐ b. suddenly
   - ☐ c. quietly

✎ _____ Number of correct answers
Enter this number on the Vocabulary graph on page 134.

Personal Response

Should Mrs. Bennett let Martin ride his bike to the school fair? Explain your answer.

_____

_____

_____

_____

20 All About Tarantulas

When people think about tarantulas, they usually don't think good things. Words like scary, ugly, and killers often come to mind. But do tarantulas really deserve this bad reputation?

Tarantulas are the largest spiders on Earth. Some of them grow to be the size of a person's hand. A few get even bigger than that. The largest ones can be the size of a dinner plate.

Maybe it's their size that makes tarantulas so fearsome. Or maybe it's their hairy bodies. Their eight beady eyes do nothing to calm the nerves, either. Then there are those two large fangs filled with venom. All in all, tarantulas look quite frightening, so they have been portrayed as aggressive killers. In movies and on TV, tarantulas have long been a symbol of death. Certain folklore may also play a part in the "bad rap" these creatures have had to live with through the ages.

The word *tarantula* comes from Taranto, a city in southern Italy, where these large spiders were first found. People once thought that a bite from this spider caused a sickness called *tarantism.* People with this illness were said to leap into the air and run wildly, making odd noises. The best cure in that day was a lively folk dance. The dance became known as the *tarantella,* which is still performed today—but not to cure disease!

The truth about tarantulas is less frightening than the myths of old would have you think. Tarantulas *do* kill with their venom, but they don't kill humans.

Their venom is designed mostly for beetles and grasshoppers. It can't disable anything larger than a mouse or bat. Tarantulas rarely bite humans. When they do, the bite is no worse than a wasp sting.

Although tarantulas do not hunt humans, they are still fascinating. Scientists have found about 800 kinds, which live mostly in warm climates. They live in the American Southwest, Europe, and Asia. In fact, they live on every continent but Antarctica.

All tarantulas share certain features. They have long, hairy legs and thick, hairy bodies. Despite their many eyes, tarantulas do not see well. In this case, more is not better. Tarantulas must rely on other senses to help them get what they need.

Most important of these is the spiders' sense of touch. Tarantulas travel by feeling their way along. They find prey by picking up vibrations made by the prey as it moves. All the hairs on the tarantulas' bodies help them sense these vibrations. The hairs move with even the slightest breeze. So when their hairs start vibrating, tarantulas know the air is swirling. That motion usually signals something nearby: dinner is on the way.

Tarantulas eat many small creatures but may themselves be eaten by other predators. Their worst enemy is the female Pepsis wasp. The Pepsis is a big wasp—the largest in the world. Because of its size and diet, it is nicknamed the "tarantula hawk."

Some people say that the more they learn about tarantulas, the more they like them. That may be why tarantulas have become popular in pet stores. More and more people are buying them. Owners praise tarantulas as being wonderful pets. ∎

✔ Enter your reading time below. Then look up your reading speed on the Words-per-Minute table on page 130.

Reading Time _____

Reading Speed _____

Enter your reading speed on the Reading Speed graph on Page 131.

Comprehension

Put an **X** in the box next to the correct answer for each question or statement. Do not look back at the selection.

1. Tarantulas are Earth's
   - ☐ a. largest spiders.
   - ☐ b. most poisonous spiders.
   - ☐ c. most popular spider.

2. Tarantulas are named after Taranto, a city in
   - ☐ a. the American Southwest.
   - ☐ b. Asia.
   - ☐ c. southern Italy.

3. What is the *tarantella?*
   - ☐ a. a sickness caused by the bite of a tarantula
   - ☐ b. a lively folk dance
   - ☐ c. a smaller kind of tarantula

4. The venom from a tarantula bite can't kill anything larger than a
   - ☐ a. human.
   - ☐ b. grasshopper.
   - ☐ c. bat.

5. Tarantulas live mostly in
   - ☐ a. warm climates.
   - ☐ b. cool climates.
   - ☐ c. wet climates.

6. Tarantulas live on every continent in the world except
   - ☐ a. Africa.
   - ☐ b. Antarctica.
   - ☐ c. North America.

7. What is the tarantula's worst enemy?
   - ☐ a. a kind of wasp
   - ☐ b. a kind of hawk
   - ☐ c. a kind of beetle

8. The more some people learn about tarantulas, the more they seem to
   - ☐ a. fear them.
   - ☐ b. think about them.
   - ☐ c. like them.

✎ _____ Number of correct answers
Enter this number on the Comprehension graph on page 132.

Critical Thinking

Put an ✘ in the box next to the best answer for each question or statement. You may look back at the selection if you'd like.

1. What was the author's purpose in writing this selection?
   - ☐ a. to warn people about tarantulas
   - ☐ b. to change people's opinions about tarantulas
   - ☐ c. to describe tarantulas and the way they live

2. Based on the selection, which of the following titles best describes tarantulas?
   - ☐ a. "Tarantulas: Not As Bad As They Look"
   - ☐ b. "Tarantulas: Large and Dangerous"
   - ☐ c. "Tarantulas: No Better Pet to Own"

3. The author feels that tarantulas have received a "bad rap" because
   - ☐ a. they are so large.
   - ☐ b. they have been wrongfully portrayed in movies and on TV.
   - ☐ c. all spiders are feared by most people.

4. As people learn more about them, you can predict that tarantulas will probably be
   - ☐ a. feared less.
   - ☐ b. feared more.
   - ☐ c. the subject of more movies.

5. Tarantulas must rely most on their sense of touch because they
   - ☐ a. have no sense of hearing.
   - ☐ b. have a poor sense of smell.
   - ☐ c. do not see well.

6. Which of the following is a statement of opinion rather than fact?
   - ☐ a. The Pepsis is a big wasp—the largest in the world.
   - ☐ b. Maybe it's their size that makes tarantulas so fearsome.
   - ☐ c. Tarantulas *do* kill with their venom, but they don't kill humans.

7. The bite of a tarantula is most like the
   - ☐ a. sting of a wasp.
   - ☐ b. bite of a rattlesnake.
   - ☐ c. sting of a jellyfish.

8. The best word to describe the author's feeling towards tarantulas is
   - ☐ a. fear.
   - ☐ b. excitement.
   - ☐ c. pity.

✎ _____ **Number of correct answers**
Enter this number on the Critical Thinking graph on page 133.

Vocabulary

Each numbered sentence contains an underlined word from the selection. Following are three definitions. Put an ✘ in the box next to the best meaning of the word as it is used in the sentence

1. Maybe it's their size that makes tarantulas so <u>fearsome</u>.
   - ☐ a. scary
   - ☐ b. huge
   - ☐ c. afraid

2. All in all, tarantulas look quite frightening, so they have been <u>portrayed</u> as aggressive killers.
   - ☐ a. mostly ignored
   - ☐ b. closely watched
   - ☐ c. presented

3. Certain <u>folklore</u> may also play a part in the "bad rap" these creatures have had to live with.
   - ☐ a. untrue stories
   - ☐ b. old families
   - ☐ c. beliefs of a people

4. Their venom is <u>designed</u> mostly for beetles and grasshoppers.
   - ☐ a. intended
   - ☐ b. saved
   - ☐ c. produced

5. It can't <u>disable</u> anything larger than a mouse or a bat.
   - ☐ a. cripple
   - ☐ b. eat
   - ☐ c. carry

6. Although tarantulas do not hunt humans, they are still <u>fascinating</u>.
   - ☐ a. difficult to find
   - ☐ b. most interesting
   - ☐ c. very unusual

7. All the hairs on the tarantulas' bodies help them <u>sense</u> these vibrations.
   - ☐ a. listen to
   - ☐ b. be aware of
   - ☐ c. see

8. Tarantulas eat many small creatures but may themselves be eaten by other <u>predators</u>.
   - ☐ a. animals that kill other animals
   - ☐ b. larger animals
   - ☐ c. fiercer animals

✎ _____ **Number of correct answers**
Enter this number on the Vocabulary graph on page 134.

Personal Response

What surprising facts did you learn about the tarantula in this selection?

_____

_____

_____

_____

✎ **Check Your Progress**
Study the graphs you completed for Lessons 11–20 and answer the How Am I Doing? questions on page 136.

21 | The Enormous Egg

by Oliver Butterworth

In this passage a family gathers around to look at an egg one of their hens laid. Nothing unusual about that. But the size of the egg is unusual—very unusual. And what hatches from the egg is much more than unusual. It's incredible!

Dr. Ziemer arrived while we were still staring at the thing in the nest. He jumped out of his car and came running out to us in the backyard. He was wearing a red bathrobe over his pajamas, and he looked pretty excited.

He ran up to the nest and looked in. His eyes opened up wide and he knelt down on the ground and stared and stared and stared. After a long while he said softly, "That's it. By George, that's just what it is." Then he stared for another long time and finally he shook his head and said, "It can't be true, but there it is."

He got up off his knees and looked around at us. His eyes were just sparkling, he was so excited. He put his hand on my shoulder, and I could feel he was quivering. "An amazing thing's happened," he said, in a kind of whisper. "I don't know how to account for it. It must be some sort of freak biological mix-up that might happen once in a thousand years."

"But what is it?" I asked.

Dr. Ziemer turned and pointed a trembling finger at the nest. "Believe it or not, you people have hatched out a *dinosaur.*"

We just looked at him.

"Sounds incredible, I know," he said, "and I can't explain it, but there it is. I've

seen too many Triceratops skulls to be mistaken about this one."

"But—but how could it be a dinosaur?" Pop asked.

"Goodness gracious!" Mom spluttered. "And right here in our backyard. It doesn't seem hardly right. And on a Sunday, too."

Cynthia was pretty interested by now, and kept peeking into the nest and making faces, the way she did when Pop brought a bowl of frogs' legs into the kitchen one time. I guess girls just naturally don't like crawly things too much. To tell the truth, I don't either sometimes, but this thing that had just hatched out looked kind of cute to me. Maybe that was because I had taken care of the egg so long. I felt as if the little dinosaur was almost one of the family.

We stood around for a long while looking at the strange new thing on the nest, trying to let the idea soak in that we had a dinosaur. After Dr. Ziemer calmed down a little, he and Pop tightened up the chicken wire to make sure the little animal wasn't going to crawl out. Dr. Ziemer watched the poor old hen for a time, and then he wondered if perhaps she ought not to be taken out before she went out of her mind. Pop figured that it might be a good idea and he picked her up and put her outside the pen. She acted a little dazed at first, but pretty soon she followed the other hens and began scratching for worms like the rest of them.

"I've never seen such a surprised hen in my life," Dr. Ziemer said. ■

✔ **Enter your reading time below. Then look up your reading speed on the Words-per-Minute table on page 130.**

Reading Time _____

Reading Speed _____

Enter your reading speed on the Reading Speed graph on page 131.

Comprehension

Put an **X** in the box next to the correct answer for each question or statement. Do not look back at the selection.

1. When Dr. Ziemer arrived, he was wearing a
   ☐ a. long coat and pajamas.
   ☐ b. bathrobe and pajamas.
   ☐ c. sweater and pants.

2. Dr. Ziemer was very
   ☐ a. excited.
   ☐ b. disappointed.
   ☐ c. annoyed.

3. The action in this story takes place
   ☐ a. at a zoo.
   ☐ b. on a chicken farm.
   ☐ c. in a backyard.

4. What did Dr. Ziemer find in the nest?
   ☐ a. a rooster
   ☐ b. a chick
   ☐ c. a dinosaur

5. On what day was the discovery made?
   ☐ a. Friday
   ☐ b. Saturday
   ☐ c. Sunday

6. To make sure the animal wouldn't get away, Dr. Ziemer and Pop
   ☐ a. tightened the chicken wire around the nest.
   ☐ b. tied the animal to a post.
   ☐ c. put the animal in the house.

7. Who's idea was it to take the hen out of the nest?
   ☐ a. Dr. Ziemer's
   ☐ b. Pop's
   ☐ c. Cynthia's

8. When put outside the nest, the hen first acted
   ☐ a. frightened.
   ☐ b. dazed.
   ☐ c. hungry.

✎ _____ **Number of correct answers**
Enter this number on the Comprehension graph on page 132.

Critical Thinking

Put an **X** in the box next to the best answer for each question or statement. You may look back at the selection if you'd like.

1. The author intended this story to be
   ☐ a. funny.
   ☐ b. sad.
   ☐ c. serious.

2. Who is telling the story?
   - ☐ a. Dr. Ziemer
   - ☐ b. Cynthia's brother
   - ☐ c. Pop

3. The fact that the storyteller considers the creature "almost one of the family" shows his
   - ☐ a. desire to have a little brother.
   - ☐ b. dislike for pets.
   - ☐ c. love for the animal.

4. Which word best describes how the family feels when they learn what kind of animal they have?
   - ☐ a. frightened
   - ☐ b. amused
   - ☐ c. shocked

5. Pop took the old hen out of the nest because Dr. Ziemer thought she might
   - ☐ a. go out of her mind.
   - ☐ b. hatch more eggs.
   - ☐ c. harm the creature.

6. Which of the following is a statement of opinion rather than fact?
   - ☐ a. I guess girls just naturally don't like crawly things too much.
   - ☐ b. Dr. Ziemer turned and pointed a trembling finger at the nest.
   - ☐ c. "I've never seen such a surprised hen in my life."

7. Which of the following does *not* fit with the other two?
   - ☐ a. dinosaur
   - ☐ b. Triceratops
   - ☐ c. hen

8. Which is the best summary of this selection?
   - ☐ a. A scientist discovers that a dinosaur has been hatched from a hen's egg. He has the hen removed from the nest. Then to prevent the dinosaur from crawling out, he tightens a chicken wire fence that is around the nest.
   - ☐ b. A scientist comes to examine a large egg that's been hatched by a family's backyard hen. He discovers it contains a dinosaur. The discovery excites him, shocks the family, and dazes the hen.
   - ☐ c. A scientist, dressed in a bathrobe and pajamas, comes to examine a recently hatched egg. He's surprised to find it contains a dinosaur. The family who owns the hen is delighted to have a new member of the family.

✎ _____ **Number of correct answers**
Enter this number on the Critical Thinking graph on page 133.

Vocabulary

Each numbered sentence contains an underlined word from the selection. Following are three definitions. Put an **X** in the box next to the best meaning of the word as it is used in the sentence.

1. His eyes were just <u>sparkling</u>, he was so excited.
   - ☐ a. cold and hard
   - ☐ b. bright and lively
   - ☐ c. sleepy and dull

2. He put his hand on my shoulder, and I could feel he was <u>quivering</u>.
   - ☐ a. thinking
   - ☐ b. shaking
   - ☐ c. ready to run

3. It must be some sort of freak <u>biological</u> mix-up.
   - ☐ a. having to do with legal matters
   - ☐ b. having to do with family relationships
   - ☐ c. having to do with living things

4. "Goodness gracious!" Mom <u>spluttered</u>.
   - ☐ a. spoke in a confused way
   - ☐ b. shouted loudly
   - ☐ c. whispered loudly

5. "Sounds <u>incredible</u>, I know," he said, "and I can't explain it."
   - ☐ a. common
   - ☐ b. reasonable
   - ☐ c. unbelievable

6. "I've seen too many Triceratops <u>skulls</u> to be mistaken about this one."
   - ☐ a. shells
   - ☐ b. feet
   - ☐ c. head bones

7. Dr. Ziemer turned and pointed a <u>trembling</u> finger at the nest.
   - ☐ a. bleeding
   - ☐ b. shaking
   - ☐ c. unmoving

8. She acted a little <u>dazed</u> at first, but pretty soon she followed the other hens.
   - ☐ a. confused
   - ☐ b. unhappy
   - ☐ c. excited

✎ _____ **Number of correct answers**
Enter this number on the Vocabulary graph on page 134.

Personal Response

Suppose you are a reporter covering the story of the dinosaur that hatched from the hen's egg. Write a headline and the first few sentences of your story.

_____
_____
_____
_____
_____

22 | Mount Washington: Small but Deadly

Mount Washington seems like such a nice little mountain. But don't let it fool you. It's often been called the most dangerous small mountain in the world.

Mount Washington, located in the state of New Hampshire, is 6,288 feet high. That height isn't too impressive when you realize that hundreds of mountains are much higher than that. Mount Whitney, in California, is more than twice as high. Mount McKinley, in Alaska, is more than three times as high. And Mount Everest, on the continent of Asia, is nearly five times as high.

Yet no one should take Mount Washington for granted. Those who do could pay a high price for their mistake. More than 100 people have perished on Mount Washington. The trails on the way up the mountain are dotted with little markers. These markers describe when and how a death occurred at each spot.

Every so often, the weather is good at the top of Mount Washington. But sunshine can't be counted on. The weather is almost always nasty. In fact, many people in New Hampshire say that Mount Washington has the world's worst weather. Although that claim is open to debate, everyone agrees that the weather at the peak is nearly always inclement.

A look at some of the numbers will show the reason. The highest wind speed ever recorded on Earth was on Mount Washington. It happened on April 12, 1934, when the wind gusted at 231 miles per hour.

On average, winds of hurricane force—or winds of more than 74 miles per hour—rise up every third day. Nature once piled 566 inches of snow on top of Mount Washington in one winter alone. In addition, it is almost always cold on the mountain. Below-zero temperatures are common. When the high winds are added to the bitter cold, the weather on Mount Washington rivals that in Antarctica. When the wind finally diminishes, a fog as thick as pea soup usually rolls in.

Even worse, the weather is not predictable. Things might look fine from the lodge at the base of the mountain. But on top, the weather can change in the blink of an eye. That is why so many hikers—even hardy ones—die on the mountain. They are not prepared for the worst.

Mount Washington's top 1,500 feet or so lie above the timberline. Once there, a person has no protection from the weather. A sudden storm can appear out of nowhere. Blinding snow and cold can easily kill people.

A driving mountain rain can kill people too. A cold summer rain may be the greatest danger of all, for rain soaks through clothing faster than snow does. When heat is drained from a person's body, the result is a condition called *hypothermia*. As the body loses heat, the brain slows down. The person can no longer think clearly and becomes confused and dazed. He or she may fall down and never get up again.

Although visitors must be cautious when they hike Mount Washington, it is still a great mountain. On a clear day—which is quite rare—a person can see 100 miles from the top. ■

✔ Enter your reading time below. Then look up your reading speed on the Words-per-Minute table on page 130.

Reading Time _____

Reading Speed _____
Enter your reading speed on the Reading Speed graph on page 131.

Comprehension

Put an **X** in the box next to the correct answer for each question or statement. Do not look back at the selection.

1. Mount Washington is located in
   - ☐ a. Alaska.
   - ☐ b. California.
   - ☐ c. New Hampshire.

2. How high is Mount Washington?
   - ☐ a. 4,000 feet
   - ☐ b. 6,000 feet
   - ☐ c. 8,000 feet

3. How many people have died on Mount Washington?
   - ☐ a. fewer than 100
   - ☐ b. more than 100
   - ☐ c. more than 200

4. How often is the weather good at the top of Mount Washington?
   - ☐ a. never
   - ☐ b. often
   - ☐ c. not very often

5. Winds are considered to be of hurricane force when they reach
   - ☐ a. 231 miles per hour.
   - ☐ b. 110 miles per hour.
   - ☐ c. 74 miles per hour.

6. Mt. Washington's high winds and bitter cold rival the weather in
   - ☐ a. Alaska.
   - ☐ b. Antarctica.
   - ☐ c. Asia.

7. The greatest danger of all to visitors on Mount Washington may be
   - ☐ a. a cold summer rain.
   - ☐ b. hurricane-force winds.
   - ☐ c. unmarked trails.

8. How far is it possible to see from the top of Mount Washington?
   - ☐ a. 25 miles
   - ☐ b. 50 miles
   - ☐ c. 100 miles

✎ _____ **Number of correct answers**
Enter this number on the Comprehension graph on page 132.

Critical Thinking

Put an **X** in the box next to the best answer for each question or statement. You may look back at the selection if you'd like.

1. The author's main purpose was to
   - ☐ a. persuade you not to go hiking on Mount Washington.
   - ☐ b. inform you about the dangerous weather conditions on Mount Washington.
   - ☐ c. persuade you that Mount Washington is a great mountain with a wonderful view from its top.

2. Which is the most important idea about Mount Washington?
   - ☐ a. It is small compared to hundreds of other mountains.
   - ☐ b. The weather at the top is nearly always bad.
   - ☐ c. Despite its small size, it is a dangerous mountain.

3. Why should hikers be especially careful on the top 1,500 feet of the mountain?
   - ☐ a. There is no protection from the weather.
   - ☐ b. The thin air makes breathing difficult.
   - ☐ c. Rock slides occur sometimes.

4. Which of these mountains is the highest?
   - ☐ a. Mount Whitney in California
   - ☐ b. Mount Everest in Asia
   - ☐ c. Mount McKinley in Alaska

5. Based on this selection, you can predict that probably
   - ☐ a. hiking will not be allowed on Mount Washington.
   - ☐ b. more people will die hiking on Mount Washington.
   - ☐ c. the weather will get much better on Mount Washington.

6. A condition known as *hypothermia* results when
   - ☐ a. people hike too long.
   - ☐ b. heat is drained from a person's body.
   - ☐ c. temperatures drop below zero.

7. Which of the following is a statement of opinion rather than fact?
   - ☐ a. The highest wind speed ever recorded on Earth was on Mount Washington.
   - ☐ b. Mount Washington's top 1,500 feet or so lie above the timberline.
   - ☐ c. A cold summer rain may be the greatest danger of all.

8. The best advice to give hikers about to climb Mount Washington is
   - ☐ a. wear warm clothing at all times.
   - ☐ b. hike only in the summer.
   - ☐ c. be prepared for the worst.

✎ _____ **Number of correct answers**
Enter this number on the Critical Thinking graph on page 133.

Vocabulary

Each numbered sentence contains an underlined word from the selection. Following are three definitions. Put an **X** in the box next to the best meaning for the word as it is used in the sentence.

1. More than 100 people have <u>perished</u> on Mount Washington.
   - ☐ a. climbed
   - ☐ b. died
   - ☐ c. gotten lost

2. These markers describe when and how a death <u>occurred</u> at each spot.
   - ☐ a. was reported
   - ☐ b. took place
   - ☐ c. was remembered

3. Everyone agrees that the weather at the peak is nearly always <u>inclement</u>.
   - ☐ a. stormy
   - ☐ b. cloudy
   - ☐ c. uncertain

4. When the high winds are added to the bitter cold, the weather on Mount Washington <u>rivals</u> that in Antarctica.
   - ☐ a. is equal to
   - ☐ b. is worse than
   - ☐ c. is better than

5. When the wind finally <u>diminishes</u>, a fog as thick as pea soup usually rolls in.
   - ☐ a. grows stronger
   - ☐ b. turns warmer
   - ☐ c. dies down

6. That is why many hikers—even <u>hardy</u> ones—die on the mountain.
   - ☐ a. strong
   - ☐ b. older
   - ☐ c. trained

7. Once there, a person has no <u>protection</u> from the weather.
   - ☐ a. help
   - ☐ b. shelter
   - ☐ c. warning

8. Although visitors must be <u>cautious</u> when they hike Mount Washington, it is still a great mountain.
   - ☐ a. curious
   - ☐ b. good hikers
   - ☐ c. careful

✎ _____ **Number of correct answers**
Enter this number on the Vocabulary graph on page 134.

Personal Response

What advice would you give to a friend who was planning to hike on Mount Washington next summer?

_____

_____

_____

_____

23 | Paul Bunyan and His Boyhood

by Dell J. McCormick

Paul Bunyan is a name known by many—especially in the great North Woods of America. Perhaps you've read or heard a tale or two about him. In this selection, you'll learn what this great woodsman was like when he was a young boy.

Many tales are told of Paul Bunyan the giant woodsman. Mightiest hero of the North Woods! A man of great size and strength who was taller than the trees of the forest. He had such strength in his huge arms that they say he could take the tallest pine tree and break it in two with his bare hands. They tell of his mighty deeds and strange adventures from Maine to California.

He could outrun the swiftest deer, and cross the widest river in one great stride! Even today lumberjacks who work in the woods find small lakes and point them out saying:

"Those are the footprints of Paul Bunyan that have been filled with water."

A giant logger was Paul and he chopped down whole forests in a single day. And he and his woodsmen logged off North Dakota in a single month! His axe was as wide as a barn door and had a great oak tree for a handle. It took six full-grown men to lift it!

They say that he was born in Maine and even as a baby he was so large that his mother and father had to have fourteen cows to supply milk for his porridge. Every morning when they looked at him he had grown two feet taller. They built a huge cradle for Paul and floated it in the ocean off the coast of Maine. The ocean waves would rock him to sleep.

One day he started bouncing up and down in his cradle and started a seventy-foot tidal wave that washed away towns and villages. After that Paul's folks gave up the idea of a floating cradle and took Paul with them into the Maine woods. Here they felt he could be kept out of mischief.

Paul spent his boyhood in the woods and helped his father cut down trees. They sawed the trees into logs and tied them together into large rafts, which were floated down the river to the sawmills. Even as a boy he had the strength of 12 men and could ride a raft through the wildest rapids in the river.

One day the man at the sawmill refused to buy the logs. They were too large for his mill to cut up into lumber. So Paul chained them together again and pulled the raft back up the river to his father's camp. Imagine his dad's surprise to see young Paul wading up the river towing the great raft of logs behind him!

Everybody liked young Paul, and for miles around they told of his great feats of strength. Once he took an iron crowbar and bent it into a safety pin to hold together a rip in his trousers. Another time he came to the end of the field he was plowing with two oxen and having no room to turn the plow and oxen around, picked up the plow, oxen and all, and turned them around to start back the other way. ■

_____

✔ Enter your reading time below. Then look up your reading speed on the Words-per-Minute table on page 130.

   Reading Time _____

   Reading Speed _____
Enter your reading speed on the Reading Speed graph on page 131.

_____

Comprehension

Put an **X** in the box next to the correct answer for each question or statement. Do not look back at the selection.

1. Even today, some lumberjacks say that some lakes are
   - ☐ a. Paul Bunyan's supply of drinking water.
   - ☐ b. Paul Bunyan's footprints filled with water.
   - ☐ c. swimming pools for Paul Bunyan.

2. Paul Bunyan and his woodsmen finished cutting all the trees in North Dakota into logs in a single
   - ☐ a. year.
   - ☐ b. day.
   - ☐ c. month.

3. What did Paul use for an axe handle?
   - ☐ a. a thick log
   - ☐ b. a long board
   - ☐ c. a great oak tree

4. People say Paul Bunyan was born in
   - ☐ a. California.
   - ☐ b. Maine.
   - ☐ c. North Dakota.

5. When Paul was a baby, how much did he grow each day?
   - ☐ a. two inches
   - ☐ b. two feet
   - ☐ c. one foot

6. Even when he was a boy, Paul had the strength of
   - ☐ a. fourteen cows.
   - ☐ b. six men.
   - ☐ c. twelve men.

7. Why did the man at the sawmill refuse to buy Paul's logs?
   - ☐ a. They were too large to cut.
   - ☐ b. There were too many.
   - ☐ c. There weren't enough.

8. How did everybody feel about young Paul?
   - ☐ a. They liked him.
   - ☐ b. They were afraid of him.
   - ☐ c. They thought he showed off too much.

_____

✎ _____ **Number of correct answers**
Enter this number on the Comprehension graph on page 132.

98

Critical Thinking

Put an ☒ in the box next to the best answer for each question or statement. You may look back at the selection if you'd like.

1. The author's main purpose in writing this story was to
   - ☐ a. entertain you with a good story.
   - ☐ b. inform you about the logging business.
   - ☐ c. persuade you that Paul Bunyan was a real person.

2. The feeling the author expresses in this selection is
   - ☐ a. serious.
   - ☐ b. humorous.
   - ☐ c. worried.

3. After reading this selection, you can conclude that Paul Bunyan
   - ☐ a. lived a long time ago.
   - ☐ b. was the strongest man in the country.
   - ☐ c. was not a real person.

4. Based on the selection, you can predict that young Paul will probably
   - ☐ a. stop logging.
   - ☐ b. continue to grow.
   - ☐ c. stay in Maine.

5. Why did Paul's folks give up the idea of floating Paul on the ocean in his cradle?
   - ☐ a. He almost drowned.
   - ☐ b. He started a tidal wave.
   - ☐ c. He couldn't sleep.

6. Based on the selection, which of the following is a statement of opinion rather than fact?
   - ☐ a. Paul Bunyan was the mightiest hero.
   - ☐ b. Many tales are told of Paul Bunyan.
   - ☐ c. They say he was born in Maine.

7. Which of the following did Paul do last?
   - ☐ a. helped log off North Dakota
   - ☐ b. started a tidal wave
   - ☐ c. towed a raft of logs up a river

8. This selection and stories like it are best described as
   - ☐ a. folk tales.
   - ☐ b. realistic stories.
   - ☐ c. mystery stories.

✎ _____ **Number of correct answers** Enter this number on the Critical Thinking graph on page 133.

Vocabulary

Each numbered sentence contains an underlined word from the selection. Following are three definitions. Put an ☒ in the box next to the best meaning of the word as it is used in the sentence.

1. They tell of his mighty <u>deeds</u> and strange adventures.
   - ☐ a. axes
   - ☐ b. acts
   - ☐ c. muscles

2. He could outrun the swiftest deer, and cross the wildest river in one great stride!
   - ☐ a. step
   - ☐ b. swing
   - ☐ c. crawl

3. His mother and father had to have fourteen cows to supply milk for his porridge.
   - ☐ a. cereal
   - ☐ b. bottle
   - ☐ c. loggers

4. Here they felt he could be kept out of mischief.
   - ☐ a. the deep woods
   - ☐ b. bad company
   - ☐ c. behavior that causes trouble

5. He had the strength of twelve men and could ride a raft through the wildest rapids in the river.
   - ☐ a. freshwater fish
   - ☐ b. fast-moving water
   - ☐ c. floating logs

6. They were too large for his mill to cut up into lumber.
   - ☐ a. logs
   - ☐ b. boards
   - ☐ c. sticks

7. Imagine his dad's surprise to see young Paul wading up the river towing the great raft of logs behind him!
   - ☐ a. running
   - ☐ b. swimming
   - ☐ c. walking

8. For miles around they told of his great feats of strength.
   - ☐ a. daring acts
   - ☐ b. stories
   - ☐ c. daily practices

✎ _____ Number of correct answers
Enter this number on the Vocabulary graph on page 134.

Personal Response

The story you just read is a tall tale. A tall tale is a story about impossible or exaggerated happenings. When a person exaggerates, he or she goes beyond the truth. Do you think a lie and an exaggeration are the same or different? Explain

_____

_____

The author uses several exaggerations in describing Paul's amazing deeds. Using exaggeration, describe two more deeds that Paul might have done.

_____

_____

24 Birth of an Island

by Millicent E. Selsam

There are thousands of islands in the oceans of the world. You may or may not find that fact interesting. But what is definitely interesting is how they got there. This passage tells how islands form in the oceans.

Many thousands of years ago, far off in the middle of a big ocean, miles from the nearest land, a crack opened in an undersea volcano. With a rumble and a roar, an explosion of red-hot lava and burning ashes burst forth. Huge black clouds swirled to the sky. The water boiled and white steam mixed with the fiery cloud.

The hot lava piled higher and higher and spread wider and wider. In this way, slowly, an island rose up in the sea.

The hot lava cooled and stiffened into shining black rock. Hot sun beat down on the rock. Cool rains fell. Now hot, now cold, the rock split and gradually broke to pieces. In the course of time, a fine crumbly soil covered the island. Where the rock met the sea, waves dashed against it, tore away pieces, and ground them to sand.

Nothing lived on the naked soil. Not as yet. But slowly, through the years, the island became covered with green plants. And slowly, animals began to move over its beaches and hills. How did they get there?

This story will be about a tropical island surrounded by warm seas. But the way the plants and animals come to this little bit of earth in the sea is the story of how plants and animals have spread from one island to another all over the world.

Around the island the wind roared, the ocean crashed, and the birds flapped their wings. The wind, the sea, and the birds were at work bringing life to the new island.

From the land nearest the new island, the wind picked up seeds light as dust, seeds with delicate airy parachutes or silky hairs that kept them drifting through the air. And from land near and far the wind brought little spiders and other insects so light they could sail on the air currents. But the wind was also loaded with invisible clouds of living things too tiny to see. Millions of the world's smallest plants— the bacteria—floated in the air. Some of these fell on the island and multiplied. Countless dustlike cells called spores were carried by the wind. These too fell on the island and sprouted, like seeds. Some grew into algae—the simplest plants made up of single cells or thin sheets of cells. Others grew into molds. Some were the spores of ferns.

Although the wind brought so many living things to the island, only the plants could grow there at first. Only they, in sunlight, could manufacture food from the minerals of the soil, water, and the carbon dioxide of the air. While many animals landed on the island, they could find no food. A spider spun its web in vain, because there were no insects it could catch in its silky threads. Insects couldn't stay until there were plants for them to eat. So the plants had to be the pioneer life on this island. ■

✔ Enter your reading time below. Then look up your reading speed on the Words-per-Minute table on page 130.

Reading Time   _____

Reading Speed   _____

Enter your reading speed on the Reading Speed graph on page 131.

Comprehension

Put an **X** in the box next to the correct answer for each question or statement. Do not look back at the selection.

1. When did the island told about in the selection form in the ocean?
   - ☐ a. many hundreds of years ago
   - ☐ b. many thousands of years ago
   - ☐ c. many millions of years ago

2. What happened when the hot lava from the volcano cooled?
   - ☐ a. The lava turned into sand.
   - ☐ b. The lava became covered with green plants.
   - ☐ c. The lava stiffened into black rock.

3. Most of the new life is brought to the island by
   - ☐ a. ocean currents.
   - ☐ b. the wind.
   - ☐ c. animals.

4. According to the selection, plants grow from seeds and
   - ☐ a. carbon dioxide.
   - ☐ b. molds.
   - ☐ c. spores.

5. The simplest plants made up of single cells or thin sheets of cells are
   - ☐ a. algae.
   - ☐ b. bacteria.
   - ☐ c. molds.

6. What were the only things that could grow on the new island at first?
   - ☐ a. plants
   - ☐ b. animals
   - ☐ c. insects

7. Plants are the only living that
   - ☐ a. the wind carries to the islands.
   - ☐ b. can grow on lava rocks.
   - ☐ c. can live off soil, water, and air.

8. Why was it useless for a spider to spin its web on a newly-formed island?
   - ☐ a. There were no insects for it to catch.
   - ☐ b. The strong winds blew it away.
   - ☐ c. The insects were too large for the web to hold.

✎ _____ **Number of correct answers**
Enter this number on the Comprehension graph on page 132.

102

Critical Thinking

Put an **X** in the box next to the best answer for each question or statement. You may look back at the selection if you'd like.

1. The author's main purpose in writing this selection was to explain
   - ☐ a. how plants and animals spread from one island to another.
   - ☐ b. how island rock was ground into sand by waves.
   - ☐ c. what happens when an underground volcano explodes.

2. What is the most important idea in this selection?
   - ☐ a. Islands were started by underground volcanoes exploding.
   - ☐ b. Wind carries many living things to an island.
   - ☐ c. Plants are the most important life to an island.

3. Why is the wind so important in developing life on a new island?
   - ☐ a. It keeps the island cool.
   - ☐ b. It carries seeds, spores, and insects to it.
   - ☐ c. It blows away the hot ashes from the volcano.

4. Based on the selection, you can predict that probably
   - ☐ a. there will not be any more islands formed.
   - ☐ b. animal and insect life will not need plants on any new island.
   - ☐ c. any new island will, in time, have plant life.

5. If there were no plants on an island, animals and insects would
   - ☐ a. grow in number quickly.
   - ☐ b. not be able to live there.
   - ☐ c. have more space to live.

6. New islands would not be able to form in the sea without
   - ☐ a. the wind.
   - ☐ b. plant life.
   - ☐ c. undersea volcanoes.

7. In the formation of an ocean island, which event happens first?
   - ☐ a. An undersea volcano explodes.
   - ☐ b. Hot lava cools and stiffens into hard rock.
   - ☐ c. A crack opens in an undersea volcano.

8. Which statement best describes the growth of life on an island?
   - ☐ a. New islands are formed with enough food for all kinds of life.
   - ☐ b. Life forms on a new island in stages.
   - ☐ c. Only plant life can live on a new island.

✎ _____ **Number of correct answers**
Enter this number on the Critical Thinking graph on page 133.

Vocabulary

Each numbered sentence contains an underlined word or phrase from the selection. Following are three definitions. Put an X in the box next to the best meaning of the word as it is used in the sentence.

1. Huge black clouds swirled to the sky.
   - ☐ a. twisted up
   - ☐ b. fell down
   - ☐ c. jumped over

2. The hot lava cooled and stiffened into shining black rock.
   - ☐ a. melted rock
   - ☐ b. clouds of steam
   - ☐ c. powdery ashes

3. Where the rock met the sea, waves dashed against it, tore away pieces, and ground them to sand.
   - ☐ a. hit roughly
   - ☐ b. ran quickly
   - ☐ c. rolled peacefully

4. Plants and animals have spread from one island to another all over the world.
   - ☐ a. scattered around
   - ☐ b. covered with a thin layer
   - ☐ c. vanished forever

5. The wind picked up seeds light as dust, seeds with delicate airy parachutes.
   - ☐ a. prickly
   - ☐ b. heavy and thick
   - ☐ c. thin and easily torn

6. The wind brought little spiders and other insects so light they could sail on the air currents.
   - ☐ a. heights
   - ☐ b. flows
   - ☐ c. pockets

7. Spores were carried by the wind. These too fell on the island and sprouted, like seeds.
   - ☐ a. bounced
   - ☐ b. blew away
   - ☐ c. began to grow

8. A spider spun its web in vain, because there were no insects it could catch in its silky threads.
   - ☐ a. with pride
   - ☐ b. without success
   - ☐ c. with help

✎ _____ **Number of correct answers**
Enter this number on the Vocabulary graph on page 134.

Personal Response

What was the most surprising or interesting thing you learned from this selection?

_____

_____

_____

_____

25 | Iditarod: The Last Great Race on Earth

Imagine racing over 1,000 miles on a sled pulled by dogs through wild country, in stormy, bitter-cold weather. You have just imagined the Iditarod.

Iditarod racers can be tall or short, young or old, men or women. There's only one thing they cannot be: cowards. If they are, they will never survive this grueling 1,160-mile race.

In the Iditarod, each racer travels alone on a sled pulled by dogs. The idea is to get from one end of Alaska to the other as fast as possible. That means all the racers—or mushers, as they are called— push themselves and their dogs to the limit. Sometimes dogs die along the way. Mushers know that they, too, might die. Still, every year, people return to run this "Last Great Race on Earth."

The race begins in the city of Anchorage. Mushers harness their best 15 or 20 sled dogs. They jump onto sleds packed with food and other supplies. Then they head out. The race course follows an old mail route that used to pass through Alaska's mining towns. But since the towns are mostly abandoned now, the race is one long trek through the wilderness. Mushers stop at 18 checkpoints along the way. Otherwise, they have no contact with the outside world until they reach the finish line in Nome.

With luck, the first hours of the race go smoothly. Sooner or later, though, trouble is bound to arise. The dogs may stumble on rough ground, cutting their paws on razor-sharp slivers of ice. Or the dogs might make a wrong turn. Then a musher may meander miles off the trail. Frozen lakes and rivers can also spell disaster. If the ice is not thick enough, the entire team can fall through, pulling the musher into the icy water. If that happens, there is little chance of getting out alive.

Then there are the storms. Four-time Iditarod winner Susan Butcher knows all about storms. She once hit a blizzard that left 30-foot high snowdrifts.

Even if mushers avoid blizzards, there is no way to avoid the bitter cold. Temperatures on the trail can drop to 50 or 60 degrees below zero. In weather like that, frostbite sets in quickly.

Certain parts of the trail hold special hazards. Farewell Burn is a 92-mile stretch of burned-out forest. The winds that whip through there blow all the snow away. So the dogs must pick their way around rocks, blackened stumps, and water holes. One year, Susan Butcher's sled crashed into a tree as she raced through the Burn. Butcher and four of her dogs were hurt in the accident.

By the middle of the race, lack of sleep becomes a real issue. Many mushers begin to doze on the sled. They have to trust their dogs to keep running in the right direction. Some exhausted mushers begin to hallucinate. They begin to see things that are not there.

Dropping out of the Iditarod is not cause for shame. When things go wrong, even the best mushers have to call it quits. Still, the thrill of crossing that finish line keeps many of them going. ■

✔ **Enter your reading time below. Then look up your reading speed on the Words-per-Minute table on page 130.**

Reading Time _____

Reading Speed _____
Enter your reading speed on the Reading Speed graph on page 131.

Comprehension

Put an **X** in the box next to the correct answer for each question or statement. Do not look back at the selection.

1. The Iditarod dogsled race begins in
   □ a. Anchorage.
   □ b. Fairbanks.
   □ c. Nome.

2. The Iditarod race covers a distance of between
   □ a. 500–1,000 miles.
   □ b. 1,000–1,500 miles.
   □ c. 1,500–2,000 miles.

3. Who or what are *mushers*?
   □ a. sled dogs
   □ b. a kind of dogsled
   □ c. racers

4. Each racing sled is pulled by
   □ a. 8 or 12 dogs.
   □ b. 10 or 15 dogs.
   □ c. 15 or 20 dogs.

5. During the race, the racers must stop at
   □ a. checkpoints.
   □ b. supply stations.
   □ c. mining towns.

6. Temperatures along the trail can drop as low as
   □ a. 0 to 20 degrees below zero.
   □ b. 30 to 40 degrees below zero.
   □ c. 50 to 60 degrees below zero.

7. Farewell Burn is the name of
   □ a. a stretch of burned-out forest.
   □ b. an Iditarod racer.
   □ c. a mining town.

8. What is the one thing Iditarod racers cannot be?
   □ a. over 50 years old
   □ b. cowards
   □ c. an Eskimo

✎ _____ **Number of correct answers**
Enter this number on the Comprehension graph on page 132.

Critical Thinking

Put an **X** in the box next to the best answer for each question or statement. You may look back at the selection if you'd like.

1. The main purpose of the first paragraph is to make you understand that
   - ☐ a. both men and women can be Iditarod racers.
   - ☐ b. the Iditarod is a long and grueling race.
   - ☐ c. Iditarod racers cannot be cowards.

2. Which of the following statements best expresses the main idea of the selection?
   - ☐ a. There are few races in the world as thrilling as the Iditarod.
   - ☐ b. Despite storms, cold, and hazards along the trail, the thrill of winning keeps many Iditarod racers going.
   - ☐ c. The idea of the Iditarod is to get from one end of Alaska to the other as fast as possible.

3. From what you've read about the Iditarod, you can conclude that
   - ☐ a. the dogsled pulled by the most dogs will win.
   - ☐ b. all dogsled teams will finish the race.
   - ☐ c. many dogsled teams will quit.

4. Which does *not* fit with the other two?
   - ☐ a. Alaska
   - ☐ b. Anchorage
   - ☐ c. Nome

5. For any Iditarod dogsled race, you can predict that
   - ☐ a. very few people will line the course to watch.
   - ☐ b. large crowds will line the course to watch.
   - ☐ c. the weather will be very cold but sunny.

6. The Farewell Burn stretch is dangerous because
   - ☐ a. strong winds leave 30-foot high snowdrifts.
   - ☐ b. ice on its frozen lakes may break.
   - ☐ c. winds blow snow away uncovering rocks, stumps, and water holes.

7. Which of the following is a statement of opinion rather than fact?
   - ☐ a. In the Iditarod, each racer travels alone on a sled pulled by dogs.
   - ☐ b. Mushers stop at 18 checkpoints along the way.
   - ☐ c. Dropping out of the Iditarod is not a cause for shame.

8. Which word best describes a racer in the Iditarod?
   - ☐ a. strong
   - ☐ b. skillful
   - ☐ c. courageous

✎ _____ **Number of correct answers**
Enter this number on the Critical Thinking graph on page 133.

Vocabulary

Each numbered sentence contains an underlined word from the selection. Following are three definitions. Put an **X** in the box next to the best meaning of the word as it is used in the sentence.

1. They will never survive this <u>grueling</u> 1,160-mile race.
   - ☐ a. restful
   - ☐ b. tiring
   - ☐ c. lengthy

2. But since then, the towns have been <u>abandoned</u>.
   - ☐ a. growing
   - ☐ b. repaired
   - ☐ c. deserted

3. Now, the race is one long <u>trek</u> through the wilderness.
   - ☐ a. road
   - ☐ b. journey
   - ☐ c. thrill

4. Or the dogs might make a wrong turn. Then a musher may <u>meander</u> miles off the trail.
   - ☐ a. drive quickly
   - ☐ b. wander aimlessly
   - ☐ c. shorten

5. Even if mushers <u>avoid</u> blizzards, there is no way to avoid the bitter cold.
   - ☐ a. run into
   - ☐ b. enjoy
   - ☐ c. keep away from

6. Certain parts of the trail hold special <u>hazards</u>.
   - ☐ a. dangers
   - ☐ b. surprises
   - ☐ c. resting places

7. By the middle of the race, lack of sleep becomes a real <u>issue</u>.
   - ☐ a. problem
   - ☐ b. help
   - ☐ c. argument

8. Many mushers begin to <u>doze</u> on the sled.
   - ☐ a. jump up
   - ☐ b. sleep lightly
   - ☐ c. ride

✎ _____ **Number of correct answers**
Enter this number on the Vocabulary graph on page 134.

Personal Response

Would you ever want to race in the Iditarod? Explain why or why not.

_____

_____

_____

_____

26 | Triangle of Fear

by Henry and Melissa Billings

Ships and planes have disappeared without a trace in an area off the southeast coast of Florida. The area is known as the Bermuda Triangle. This selection offers some theories about what might have caused the disappearances.

On a calm, clear December afternoon in 1945, Flight 19 took off from the south coast of Florida on a routine Navy training mission. The five Avenger planes that made up Flight 19 would never return. Incredibly, a Martin Mariner plane sent to rescue Flight 19 was also lost without a trace.

Whenever planes or ships disappear in the infamous Bermuda Triangle, the wildest stories are heard. Many people think that the waters off the coast of Florida are the deadliest in the world. Legends tell of hundreds of ships and airplanes simply disappearing in the Bermuda Triangle.

Why is the Bermuda Triangle such a graveyard? Some say that it is a hunting ground for UFOs. According to this theory, UFOs hover above the Bermuda Triangle waiting to scoop up innocent ships and airplanes. Others claim that the area creates a time warp, causing vessels to vanish into the fourth dimension. Whatever the case, the Bermuda Triangle is made to sound like a place to avoid.

In fact, one member of Flight 19 did avoid the Triangle. He claimed he had an unexplainable feeling that something was going to go wrong. So he did not go on the mission. The rest of the crew, however, did go. The leader was Lieutenant Charles Taylor, a pilot with over 2,500 hours of flying experience.

Not long after takeoff, trouble developed. Taylor radioed the control tower. "Tower, this is an emergency. We seem to be off course. We cannot see land. Repeat, we cannot see land."

"What's your position?" the tower asked.

"We can't be sure. We seem to be lost."

"Head due west," said the tower.

"We don't know which way is west. Everything is wrong. . . strange. . . we can't be sure of any direction. Even the ocean doesn't look as it should."

Later came this message from Flight 19: "We must be about 225 miles northeast of base . . . it looks like we are. . . ."

Then silence.

A Martin Mariner flying boat was sent out immediately to rescue the Avengers. But upon entering the Triangle, it too fell silent. A massive search of the area by hundreds of boats and planes turned up nothing but water.

What's the explanation for these disappearances, which many people regard as the greatest aviation mystery of all time? To true believers in the powers of the Bermuda Triangle, the fate of the five Avengers and the Martin Mariner is just another piece of evidence proving that the Triangle is one spooky stretch of ocean.

On the other hand, there is some sentiment that there is no mystery here at all. Many believe the Avengers simply became lost, ran out of gas, crashed, and sank.

And what about the Martin Mariner flying boat that was sent to rescue Flight 19? It did not take off until after dark. Observers aboard the steamship *Gaines Mills* saw an explosion in midair. The burst of flames occurred exactly where the plane was supposed to be.

The fates of Flight 19 and the Martin Mariner continues to stir discussion. ■

✔ Enter your reading time below. Then look up your reading speed on the Words-per-Minute table on page 130.

Reading Time _____

Reading Speed _____

Enter your reading speed on the Reading Speed graph on page 131.

Comprehension

Put an **X** in the box next to the correct answer for each question or statement. Do not look back at the selection.

1. Navy Flight 19 took off from
   □ a. Bermuda.
   □ b. Florida.
   □ c. a Navy aircraft carrier.

2. How many planes made up Flight 19?
   □ a. three
   □ b. five
   □ c. seven

3. Flight 19 was on a
   □ a. training mission.
   □ b. secret mission.
   □ c. rescue mission.

4. Why did one member of Flight 19 not go on its final flight?
   □ a. He was too sick to go.
   □ b. He felt that something was going to go wrong.
   □ c. He was on military leave.

5. Trouble began to develop for Flight 19
   □ a. on their return flight.
   □ b. just before they took off.
   □ c. not long after takeoff.

6. About what problem did the leader of Flight 19 radio the control tower?
   □ a. They were running out of gas.
   □ b. They couldn't see land and were lost.
   □ c. They had run into a storm.

7. Lieutenant Charles Taylor was the
   □ a. pilot of the Martin Mariner flying boat.
   □ b. commander of the Navy base.
   □ c. leader of Flight 19.

8. What did observers aboard the steamship *Gaines Mills* see?
   □ a. a midair explosion
   □ b. several planes overhead
   □ c. a plane crash into the sea

✎ _____ Number of correct answers
Enter this number on the Comprehension graph on page 132.

Critical Thinking

Put an X in the box next to the best answer for each question or statement. You may look back at the selection if you'd like.

1. The purpose of the first paragraph is to
   - ☐ a. tell you the location where the events happened.
   - ☐ b. inform you that the selection is about Navy planes and their crews.
   - ☐ c. suggest a mystery in order to capture your interest.

2. What is the main idea of the selection?
   - ☐ a. Both Flight 19 and a Martin Mariner flying boat were lost while flying over the Bermuda Triangle.
   - ☐ b. The Bermuda Triangle may be a hunting ground for UFOs.
   - ☐ c. Because many planes and ships have disappeared without a good explanation, many people think the Bermuda Triangle has strange powers.

3. From the selection, you can conclude that
   - ☐ a. no one knows what happened to the missing Navy planes.
   - ☐ b. some mysterious force caused the disappearance of the Navy planes.
   - ☐ c. all the missing planes ran out of gas, crashed, and sank into the sea.

4. Which of the following does *not* fit?
   - ☐ a. Martin Mariner
   - ☐ b. Avenger
   - ☐ c. *Gaines Mills*

5. Which word best describes the mood or feeling of the selection?
   - ☐ a. gloomy
   - ☐ b. terrifying
   - ☐ c. mysterious

6. People think the waters off the coast of Florida are the deadliest in the world because many
   - ☐ a. hurricanes happen there.
   - ☐ b. planes and ships have disappeared there.
   - ☐ c. kinds of deadly sharks live there.

7. Which of the following is a statement of fact rather than opinion?
   - ☐ a. On a calm, clear December afternoon in 1945, Flight 19 took off.
   - ☐ b. The disappearance of the six Navy planes is the greatest aviation mystery of all time.
   - ☐ c. The waters off the coast of Florida are the deadliest in the world.

8. Which event happened first?
   - ☐ a. A Martin Mariner flying boat took off from Florida.
   - ☐ b. The leader of Flight 19 radioed the control tower.
   - ☐ c. Observers aboard the *Gaines Mills* saw an explosion in midair.

✎ _____ **Number of correct answers**
Enter this number on the Critical Thinking graph on page 133.

Vocabulary

Each numbered sentence contains an underlined word from the selection. Following are three definitions. Put an **✗** in the box next to the best meaning of the word as it is used in the sentence.

1. Flight 19 took off on a <u>routine</u> Navy training mission.
   - ☐ a. unusual
   - ☐ b. dangerous
   - ☐ c. regular

2. Whenever planes or ships disappear in the <u>infamous</u> Bermuda Triangle, the wildest stories are heard.
   - ☐ a. distant
   - ☐ b. having a bad reputation
   - ☐ c. celebrated

3. <u>Legends</u> tell of hundreds of ships and airplanes simply disappearing.
   - ☐ a. stories from the past
   - ☐ b. old sailors
   - ☐ c. newspaper articles

4. According to this <u>theory</u>, UFOs hover above the Bermuda Triangle waiting to scoop up innocent ships and airplanes.
   - ☐ a. true story
   - ☐ b. opinion
   - ☐ c. teaching

5. Not long after takeoff, trouble <u>developed</u>.
   - ☐ a. was avoided
   - ☐ b. came into being
   - ☐ c. was corrected

6. A <u>massive</u> search of the area by hundreds of boats and planes turned up nothing but water.
   - ☐ a. very big
   - ☐ b. well-advertised
   - ☐ c. huge

7. What's the explanation for these disappearances, which many people <u>regard</u> as the greatest aviation mystery of all time?
   - ☐ a. remember
   - ☐ b. think of
   - ☐ c. discuss

8. There is some <u>sentiment</u> that there is no mystery here at all.
   - ☐ a. feeling
   - ☐ b. proof
   - ☐ c. concern

✎ _____ **Number of correct answers**
Enter this number on the Vocabulary graph on page 134.

Personal Response

What do you think happened to the ships and planes that disappeared in the Bermuda Triangle?

_____

_____

_____

_____

27 | The Man and the Snake

by Ambrose Bierce

"NEVER stare into the eyes of a snake." Is this good advice, or just a ridiculous old belief? After reading this passage, you decide.

Harold Brayton, a scientist and teacher, had just returned to San Francisco from a trip to Europe where he had been doing research. He had gladly accepted the invitation of Dr. Druring, the distinguished scientist, to spend several days at his home.

It was Brayton's habit to read a bit before going to bed. And although he was a guest at the Drurings' house, he found it difficult to sleep without reading a few lines. Brayton moved to the bookcase in the guest room he was using and glanced over the books. One, in particular, caught his eye. It was an old volume whose aged leather jacket was cracking. It was entitled Morrison's *Marvels of Science.*

Brayton was curious to see what "marvels of science" passed for truth in old Morrison's day. He settled himself in a chair, flipped open the book, and came to the following passage:

The following is a fact, for many wise and learned people have reported it to be true. The eyes of this serpent have a magnetic quality. Whoever is drawn into its gaze will be unable to look away. Therefore NEVER stare into the eyes of a snake, or you will perish miserably by the creature's bite.

Brayton smiled as he read this passage. Then he muttered, "Imagine a snake's eyes having such power! Ridiculous!"

Brayton, however, could not help thinking about the words, because he was,

after all, a man of thought. As he did, Brayton lowered the book without realizing he had done so. As soon as the volume had gone below the level of his eyes, something in a corner of the room caught his attention.

What he saw in the shadow under his bed were two small points of light, about an inch apart. They might have been reflections of something in the room. He gave them little thought and resumed his reading. After reading two paragraphs more, something inside him made him lower the book, and look again toward the shadow.

The points of light were still there. They seemed to have become brighter than before and shone with a greenish glow that he had not noticed before. He thought, too, that they might have moved just a bit—were somewhat nearer.

They were still too deep in the shadow to be clearly seen, and again he went back to his reading. Suddenly, something occurred to him that startled him and made him drop the book. He arose from the chair, bent over, and stared into darkness beneath the bed. The points of light, it seemed to him, shone with even greater brightness now. His curiosity was now completely aroused. He came closer to the bed and peered under it.

He saw, in the shadow under the bed, the coils of a large serpent. The points of light were its eyes! Its head, which arose from the coils, was pointed straight toward him. The snake's eyes gazed at him. They looked deep into his own. ■

✔ **Enter your reading time below. Then look up your reading speed on the Words-per-Minute table on page 130.**

Reading Time _____

Reading Speed _____

Enter your reading speed on the Reading Speed graph on page 131.

Comprehension

Put an **✗** in the box next to the correct answer for each question or statement. Do not look back at the selection.

1. Who was Morrison?
   - ☐ a. a book author
   - ☐ b. a scientist
   - ☐ c. a teacher

2. Harold Brayton had just returned from
   - ☐ a. San Francisco.
   - ☐ b. Chicago.
   - ☐ c. Europe.

3. What had Brayton gone there for?
   - ☐ a. a vacation
   - ☐ b. to do research
   - ☐ c. to teach

4. Brayton wanted to read a bit before going to bed because
   - ☐ a. he was doing some research.
   - ☐ b. it was too early to go to bed.
   - ☐ c. he found it difficult to sleep without reading a little.

5. Brayton found a book to read in
   - ☐ a. Dr. Druring's library.
   - ☐ b. his own suitcase.
   - ☐ c. a bookcase in the guest room.

6. According to the passage Brayton read, a person who stares into a snake's eyes will
   - ☐ a. die by the snake's bite.
   - ☐ b. go crazy.
   - ☐ c. be put to sleep.

7. What first caught Brayton's attention while he was reading?
   - ☐ a. two points of light
   - ☐ b. something moving in the shadows
   - ☐ c. a soft hissing sound

8. What were the points of light under the bed?
   - ☐ a. reflections from a lamp in the room
   - ☐ b. the shiny skin of a snake
   - ☐ c. the eyes of a snake

✎ _____ **Number of correct answers**
Enter this number on the Comprehension graph on page 132.

Critical Thinking

Put an **X** in the box next to the best answer for each question or statement. You may look back at the selection if you'd like.

1. Which word best describes the mood or feeling of this selection?
   - ☐ a. peaceful
   - ☐ b. terrifying
   - ☐ c. mysterious

2. Who is telling this story?
   - ☐ a. Harold Brayton
   - ☐ b. an outside observer
   - ☐ c. Dr. Druring

3. Where was Dr. Druring's home?
   - ☐ a. Europe
   - ☐ b. San Francisco
   - ☐ c. Chicago

4. Based on what you've read, you can predict that Harold Brayton will probably
   - ☐ a. be unable to look away from the snake's eyes.
   - ☐ b. kill the snake.
   - ☐ c. ignore the snake.

5. What effect did reading the passage about the eyes of the snake have on Brayton?
   - ☐ a. He thought it could be true.
   - ☐ b. He thought it was ridiculous.
   - ☐ c. He found it boring.

6. In what way were Harold Brayton and Dr. Druring alike?
   - ☐ a. Both were scientists.
   - ☐ b. Both lived in San Francisco.
   - ☐ c. Both were teachers.

7. One question left unanswered by this story is
   - ☐ a. How did Brayton know there was a snake in the room?
   - ☐ b. Why was Brayton at Dr. Druring's home?
   - ☐ c. How did the snake come to be in the room?

8. Which of these does *not* fit with the other two?
   - ☐ a. Chicago
   - ☐ b. San Francisco
   - ☐ c. Europe

✎ _____ **Number of correct answers**
Enter this number on the Critical Thinking graph on page 133.

Vocabulary

Each numbered sentence below contains an underlined word from the selection. Following are three definitions. Put an **X** in the box next to the best meaning of the word as it is used in the sentence.

1. He had gladly <u>accepted</u> the invitation of Dr. Druring.
   - ☐ a. refused
   - ☐ b. ignored
   - ☐ c. agreed to

2. As he did, Brayton lowered the book without <u>realizing</u> he had done so.
   - ☐ a. remembering
   - ☐ b. forgetting
   - ☐ c. being aware

3. As soon as the volume had gone below the <u>level</u> of his eyes, something in a corner of the room caught his attention.
   - ☐ a. height
   - ☐ b. corner
   - ☐ c. sight

4. He gave them little thought and <u>resumed</u> his reading.
   - ☐ a. finished
   - ☐ b. delayed
   - ☐ c. began again

5. Suddenly, something occurred to him that <u>startled</u> him and made him drop the book.
   - ☐ a. amused
   - ☐ b. frightened
   - ☐ c. reminded

6. He <u>arose</u> from his chair, bent over, and stared into the darkness beneath the bed.
   - ☐ a. got up
   - ☐ b. backed away
   - ☐ c. walked

7. His curiosity was now completely <u>aroused</u>.
   - ☐ a. forgotten
   - ☐ b. awakened
   - ☐ c. spoiled

8. He came closer to the bed and <u>peered</u> under it.
   - ☐ a. crawled
   - ☐ b. pushed something
   - ☐ c. looked closely

✎ _____ **Number of correct answers**
Enter this number on the Vocabulary graph on page 134.

Personal Response

If I were the author, here's how I would end the story:

_____

_____

_____

_____

If you had been Harold Brayton, what would you have done differently?

_____

_____

_____

_____

28 | To See Half the World

by Edward Fry

Think of the world as two halves—one half being above the water; the other half being under water. In this article, the author shows how you can experience a part of that little-known underwater world.

Most people who go to places like Florida or California see only half the world. They see the half above the water. To see the other half, you must learn to snorkel.

First you have to learn to swim. It also helps to know how to float so you can rest. If you learn to float in a lake or in a swimming pool, you will easily float in the ocean because salt water holds you up better.

To snorkel, the only things you must have are a face mask and a snorkel tube. A snorkel tube is a short curved piece of plastic or rubber tubing that you put in your mouth so you can breathe while floating on your stomach. A face mask covers your eyes and nose. You can't see well under water unless your eyes are protected.

Now, to see the other half of the world under water, all you have to do is float face down with your face mask on. To breathe, just put the mouthpiece of the snorkel in your mouth. The other end of the tube will be in the air behind your head. For some reason this is scary for a lot of people. So, in the beginning, try snorkeling in shallow water where you can stand up if you get nervous. After a little while you will get used to breathing through your mouth while floating.

If a small wave should wash over the top of your snorkel tube, a little water may come down the tube. Just stop breathing for a moment and give a good hard blow. The water and air will come flying out of the tube, and you will look like a whale.

While you are floating with your face mask on you will notice that you can see the bottom and anything—plants, animals, or junk—floating in the water. If you drop money or your watch in the water a face mask will help you find it. If there are any fish or interesting shells you will see them too.

Pretty soon you will get tired of floating in one spot and will want to see more. You can swim without even raising your head. The breaststroke works just fine while floating with your snorkel and face mask on. Or you can just kick your legs and you will move. If you want to get somewhere fast put some swim fins on your feet, and you will really travel.

After a little while you may get tired of just looking at a sandy bottom. You will probably want to see some more interesting marine life. To see these plants and animals, you need to be near rocks or seaweed. Single fish or schools of fish do show up almost anywhere in the ocean, but your chances of seeing them are low. In warmer water like that in Florida, California, or Mexico there are almost always some fish near rocks, seaweed, or sunken boats.

Just looking at the rocks and seaweed under water can be a whole new seeing experience. Now you are seeing the half of the world that most people never see. ■

✔ **Enter your reading time below. Then look up your reading speed on the Words-per-Minute table on page 130.**

Reading Time _____

Reading Speed _____
Enter your reading speed on the Reading Speed graph on page 131.

Comprehension

Put an **X** in the box next to the correct answer for each question or statement. Do not look back at the selection.

1. The half of the world that most people never see is the half
   - ☐ a. below the surface of the water.
   - ☐ b. above the water.
   - ☐ c. below the equator.

2. To learn how to snorkel, you must first be able to
   - ☐ a. see under water.
   - ☐ b. float on top of the water.
   - ☐ c. swim.

3. A snorkel tube is used for
   - ☐ a. protecting your eyes.
   - ☐ b. breathing air.
   - ☐ c. helping you float on your stomach.

4. Why should you snorkel in shallow water when you first begin?
   - ☐ a. You can stand up if you get nervous.
   - ☐ b. You can see the bottom more clearly.
   - ☐ c. It's easier to float in shallow water.

5. If you get water in your snorkel tube, you should
   - ☐ a. take it off and shake it.
   - ☐ b. blow hard through the tube.
   - ☐ c. get another snorkel tube.

6. Which swimming stroke works well when you snorkel?
   - ☐ a. the backstroke
   - ☐ b. the breaststroke
   - ☐ c. the butterfly stroke

7. You will travel faster through the water if you wear
   - ☐ a. a snorkel.
   - ☐ b. swim fins.
   - ☐ c. a face mask.

8. You are more likely to see fish near
   - ☐ a. beaches.
   - ☐ b. sailboats.
   - ☐ c. seaweed.

✎ _____ **Number of correct answers**
Enter this number on the Comprehension graph on page 132.

Critical Thinking

Put an **X** in the box next to the best answer for each question or statement. You may look back at the selection if you'd like.

1. The author intended this article to be
   - ☐ a. informative.
   - ☐ b. humorous.
   - ☐ c. mysterious.

2. The main point this article makes about snorkeling is that it
   - ☐ a. can be scary and dangerous.
   - ☐ b. is best done in Florida and California.
   - ☐ c. lets you see and experience new and interesting things.

3. The author probably
   - ☐ a. has never snorkeled.
   - ☐ b. enjoys snorkeling.
   - ☐ c. prefers deep-sea diving.

4. People who enjoy snorkeling can best be described as people who
   - ☐ a. like to explore and discover new things.
   - ☐ b. like to swim under water.
   - ☐ c. prefer to swim in warm water.

5. You will almost always see fish near rocks and seaweed in places like Florida, California, or Mexico because the water is
   - ☐ a. calmer there.
   - ☐ b. clearer there.
   - ☐ c. warmer there.

6. Which of the following is a statement of opinion rather than fact?
   - ☐ a. To snorkel, the only things you must have are a face mask and a snorkel tube.
   - ☐ b. A face mask covers your eyes and nose.
   - ☐ c. Most people who go to Florida or California see only half the world.

7. Which is the best summary of this article?
   - ☐ a. Snorkeling lets you see some of the world that is under the water. By floating face down and using only a snorkeling tube to breathe and a face mask, you can see interesting new plant and animal life.
   - ☐ b. People who go to Florida or California see only the half of the world that's above water. Those who visit those places can see the other half if they learn how to snorkel.
   - ☐ c. Learning to snorkel is easy if you know how to swim. You need only to wear a face mask and use a snorkeling tube to breathe. Then all you have to do is float face down and see what's under the water.

8. Which of the following does *not* fit with the other two?
   □ a. swim fins
   □ b. seaweed
   □ c. snorkeling tube

✎ _____ Number of correct answers
Enter this number on the Critical Thinking graph on page 133.

Vocabulary

Each numbered sentence contains an underlined word from the selection. Following are three definitions. Put an **X** in the box next to the best meaning of the word as it is used in the sentence.

1. So, in the beginning, try snorkeling in very shallow water.
   □ a. very deep
   □ b. cool and clear
   □ c. not deep

2. A small wave might wash over the top of your snorkel tube.
   □ a. drown
   □ b. flow
   □ c. whisper

3. You will probably want to see some more interesting marine life.
   □ a. of the sea
   □ b. overhead
   □ c. nearby

4. The breaststroke works just fine while floating with your snorkel and face mask on.
   □ a. illness
   □ b. swimming movement
   □ c. breathing tube

5. Floating with your face mask on, you will notice that you can see the bottom and anything floating in the water.
   □ a. discover
   □ b. forget
   □ c. announce

6. Single fish or schools of fish do show up almost anywhere in the ocean.
   □ a. remains
   □ b. groups
   □ c. buildings

7. There are almost always some fish near rocks, seaweed, or sunken boats.
   □ a. fishing
   □ b. lying on the bottom
   □ c. floating on the top

8. Just looking at the rocks and seaweed under water can be a whole new kind of seeing experience.
   □ a. boat
   □ b. expert
   □ c. event

✎ _____ Number of correct answers
Enter this number on the Vocabulary graph on page 134.

Personal Response

List two things you learned about snorkeling from this article.

_____

_____

29 Hotel for Dogs

by Lois Duncan

In this passage Liz must find a home for a stray dog and her new puppies. She has a plan. But her plan is beginning to make someone feel uneasy.

"Thank goodness, it's Friday," Liz said. "This way I can spend all tomorrow over here getting them settled. Oh, Bruce, this is the most wonderful idea! Sadie and her puppies will think they're staying in a hotel!"

"Well, they had better not get too used to it," Bruce said. "As soon as the pups are old enough, we're going to find homes for every one of them and for Sadie too."

He spoke decisively to cover the fact that he was beginning to feel a little nervous. The idea had seemed so reasonable when it had first occurred to him: a vacant house with no one to tend it, four little dogs that needed a place to stay, so why not put them together for a few weeks?

The thing that was not reasonable was the way Liz was acting. In the day she had spent at home having her stomachache, she had formed a deep attachment for the group in the sewing closet. She had given them all names—Sadie for the mother and Tom, Dick, and Harry for the puppies—and she was acting as though she expected to be their mistress for the rest of her life.

"This is just an emergency thing, Liz," Bruce kept saying, as he followed her about. "This is somebody's else's property, even if they're not living here. We really shouldn't be using it at all."

"I know, I know." Liz's eyes were shining with excitement. "I think Sadie would like the pink bedroom at the front of the hotel, don't you? We can fix her a bed in one corner, and when the puppies start walking they can go exploring down the hall to the living room."

"By the time they can do that, they'll be ready to leave," Bruce said. "We should start right now trying to line up homes for them. Does your school have a bulletin board? You can pin up a sort of announcement—"

But Liz was gone again, hurrying through the kitchen to see if the faucets were working.

Liz was up at dawn the next morning and out of the house before anyone else was awake. Mrs. Walker discovered her room empty when she went to call her to breakfast.

"I can't understand it," she said in bewilderment, as she joined the rest of the family in the dining room. "Liz never gets up early if she can help it. Where in the world could she have disappeared to?"

"Perhaps she's gone to someone's house," Mr. Walker suggested. "She talks as though she had plenty of school friends she likes to play with."

"This early?" Mrs. Walker shook her head. "Nobody goes visiting before breakfast." She turned to Bruce. "Did your sister say anything to you about having plans for this morning?"

"I—I don't think so. I mean, I don't exactly remember." Bruce felt his face growing hot. He had never been able to tell a lie successfully, even a little one. ■

✔ **Enter your reading time below. Then look up your reading speed on the Words-per-Minute table on page 130.**

Reading Time   _____

Reading Speed   _____

Enter your reading speed on the Reading Speed graph on page 131.

Comprehension

Put an **X** in the box next to the correct answer for each question or statement. Do not look back at the selection.

1. Why did Liz say, "Thank goodness it's Friday"?
   - ☐ a. She could sleep late on Saturday.
   - ☐ b. She could spend all day Saturday getting the pups and their mother settled.
   - ☐ c. On Saturday she could begin to find the pups new homes.

2. After learning about Liz's plan, Bruce felt
   - ☐ a. excited.
   - ☐ b. sick.
   - ☐ c. nervous.

3. How many puppies did Sadie have?
   - ☐ a. two
   - ☐ b. three
   - ☐ c. four

4. Liz planned to keep Sadie and her puppies in
   - ☐ a. a vacant house.
   - ☐ b. a nearby hotel.
   - ☐ c. her own home.

5. Liz wanted Sadie and her puppies to stay in the
   - ☐ a. front bedroom.
   - ☐ b. living room.
   - ☐ c. basement.

6. Bruce thought Liz should begin lining up homes for Sadie and the pups by putting up an announcement on the
   - ☐ a. library bulletin board.
   - ☐ b. supermarket bulletin board.
   - ☐ c. school bulletin board.

7. Liz disappeared from the house
   - ☐ a. after dinner.
   - ☐ b. during lunch.
   - ☐ c. before breakfast.

8. Who was bewildered by Liz's disappearance?
   - ☐ a. Bruce
   - ☐ b. Mrs. Walker
   - ☐ c. Mr. Walker

✎ _____ **Number of correct answers**
Enter this number on the Comprehension graph on page 132.

Critical Thinking

Put an X in the box next to the best answer for each question or statement. You may look back at the selection if you'd like.

1. Which word best describes the mood or feeling of this selection?
   - ☐ a. serious
   - ☐ b. funny
   - ☐ c. sad

2. Liz showed her attachment to the dogs by
   - ☐ a. keeping them in the closet.
   - ☐ b. posting an announcement about them.
   - ☐ c. giving them names.

3. Which is the best word to describe the kind of person Liz is?
   - ☐ a. selfish
   - ☐ b. caring
   - ☐ c. careless

4. Which event happened first?
   - ☐ a. Mrs. Walker discovered Liz's room was empty.
   - ☐ b. Liz hurried to the kitchen to see if the faucets were working.
   - ☐ c. Liz spent the day at home with a stomachache.

5. Bruce's face began growing hot because
   - ☐ a. he had a fever.
   - ☐ b. he told a lie.
   - ☐ c. it was very warm in the dining room.

6. Which of the following is a statement of opinion rather than fact?
   - ☐ a. Liz was up at dawn the next morning.
   - ☐ b. "I think Sadie would like the pink bedroom at the front of the hotel."
   - ☐ c. "Liz never gets up early if she can help it."

7. In which way did Bruce think differently from Liz about the stray dogs?
   - ☐ a. He thought it was a good idea to help them.
   - ☐ b. He liked the dogs.
   - ☐ c. He thought they should care for the dogs only for a short time.

8. Bruce feared that Liz would
   - ☐ a. not be able to find homes for the dogs.
   - ☐ b. ask him to take care of the dogs.
   - ☐ c. abandon the dogs.

✎ _____ **Number of correct answers**
Enter this number on the Critical Thinking graph on page 133.

Vocabulary

Each numbered sentence contains an underlined word from the selection. Following are three definitions. Put an **✗** in the box next to the best meaning of the word as it is used in the sentence.

1. He spoke <u>decisively</u> to cover the fact that he was beginning to get a little nervous.
   - ☐ a. uneasily
   - ☐ b. firmly
   - ☐ c. briefly

2. The idea had seemed so <u>reasonable</u> when it had first occurred to him.
   - ☐ a. unbelievable
   - ☐ b. impossible
   - ☐ c. sensible

3. The <u>vacant</u> house had no one to tend it.
   - ☐ a. busy
   - ☐ b. sturdy
   - ☐ c. empty

4. She had formed a deep <u>attachment</u> for the group in the sewing closet.
   - ☐ a. dislike
   - ☐ b. affection
   - ☐ c. purpose

5. "You could pin up a sort of <u>announcement</u>—"
   - ☐ a. award
   - ☐ b. order
   - ☐ c. message

6. "I can't understand it," she said in <u>bewilderment</u>.
   - ☐ a. confusion
   - ☐ b. happiness
   - ☐ c. carelessness

7. "Perhaps she's gone to someone's house," Mr. Walker <u>suggested</u>.
   - ☐ a. cried
   - ☐ b. asked
   - ☐ c. proposed

8. He had never been able to tell a lie <u>successfully</u>, even a little one.
   - ☐ a. clearly
   - ☐ b. well
   - ☐ c. badly

✎ _____ **Number of correct answers**
Enter this number on the Vocabulary graph on page 134.

Personal Response

Do you approve of the way Liz is handling the situation with Sadie and her pups? Explain why or why not.

_____

_____

Has Liz acted unfairly to Bruce in any way? Explain your answer.

_____

_____

30 | Set Your Sails for Fun!

by Jennifer Albert

Sometimes people want to do something really exciting. Other times they enjoy doing something that's just plain relaxing. In this article, the author tells you about an activity that can be both exciting and relaxing—the sport of ocean sailing.

Imagine yourself gazing up at a clear blue sky, soaking up the sun's rays, and being gently rocked back and forth. You inhale fresh, clean air. You hear only the pounding of the surf in the distance. And only the lapping waves against the hull. There is absolutely nothing for miles around you except aqua-blue water.

Sailing, when done properly, can be thrilling and exhilarating. Or it can be one of the most relaxing and soothing sports there is. Sailing is one of the oldest sports.

Sailboats are designed in many different styles for varying purposes. Some people want to race, and so need a sleeker design, while others may want to simply cruise along at a slow pace.

There is a whole language that goes along with sailing, and a sailor must know it. For example, on a common sailboat called a *sloop*, there are at least three different "sheets" or lines used to control the sails. There is a name for every line. The sailor must know each one.

Let's run through a day of ocean sailing. Usually, the day begins early so you can have time to set up and get out on the water while it's still smooth.

Setting up requires teamwork. Sails must be brought out, battens (long, rulerlike sticks) are put into the sails for

support, the jib (forward sail) is attached to the forestay, and the mainsail is fed into a groove cut on the mast. Food, water, and other supplies are brought on board. Soon the boat is ready to sail.

Finally you cast off the dock lines, come aboard, and you're off! Careful maneuvering is necessary inside the breakwater where there are usually quite a few other boats. But after you're out on the ocean, you're free!

The jib is hoisted (raised) at about this time, or sometimes before leaving the dock, depending on the wind conditions. The captain pulls her into a nice "reach," with the sail at right angles to the wind. Then you can sit back, relax, and get some sun.

There are often several good hours of sailing around on the ocean. It all depends on the wind conditions. The wind determines where you go, how many times you need to change direction, and how long you can stay out. Because the wind is a variable, careful planning is needed to allow enough time to reach your destination before dark. It is best not to be out on the ocean fighting your way back at or after sunset.

Coming in an hour or so before dusk also gives you time to dock the boat, take down the sails, pack up everything, and leave the boat "shipshape" before heading home.

At the end of the day, you feel relaxed, warm from the sun, and sleepy. You'll look back on the day and you'll probably remember each picture printed in your mind. You'll remember the sun on the waves, the sea gulls, the blue sky, and the water all around. ■

✔ **Enter your reading time below. Then look up your reading speed on the Words-per-Minute table on page 130.**

Reading Time   _____

Reading Speed   _____

Enter your reading speed on the Reading Speed graph on page 131.

Comprehension

Put an **X** in the box next to the correct answer for each question or statement. Do not look back at the selection.

1. The author describes sailing as being
   - ☐ a. difficult and dangerous.
   - ☐ b. exhilarating or soothing.
   - ☐ c. dull and tiring.

2. According to the article, sailing is
   - ☐ a. one of the most popular sports.
   - ☐ b. one of the most expensive sports.
   - ☐ c. one of the oldest sports.

3. A sloop is a
   - ☐ a. common type of sailboat.
   - ☐ b. type of sail used only for racing.
   - ☐ c. small sailboat for beginners.

4. What is the jib?
   - ☐ a. the largest sail
   - ☐ b. the mainsail
   - ☐ c. the forward sail

5. What determines when the jib is raised?
   - ☐ a. the wind conditions
   - ☐ b. the depth of the water
   - ☐ c. the size of the sailboat

6. Where is it necessary to maneuver the sailboat with special care?
   - ☐ a. inside the breakwater
   - ☐ b. out on the ocean
   - ☐ c. at the entrance to the harbor

7. When the captain pulls the sailboat into a nice "reach," the sail is
   - ☐ a. pointed directly into the wind.
   - ☐ b. at right angles to the wind.
   - ☐ c. pulled in toward the sailboat.

8. When is it best not to be out in the ocean in a sailboat?
   - ☐ a. before noon
   - ☐ b. late afternoon
   - ☐ c. after sunset

✎ _____ **Number of correct answers**
Enter this number on the Comprehension graph on page 132.

Critical Thinking

Put an X in the box next to the best answer for each question or statement. You may look back at the selection if you'd like.

1. The author uses the first paragraph to
   ☐ a. make you wonder what place she is talking about.
   ☐ b. relax you and make you wonder what's next.
   ☐ c. persuade you to visit the ocean.

2. Which is the main idea of the article?
   ☐ a. Sailing can be dangerous after sunset.
   ☐ b. Sailing is a very enjoyable sport.
   ☐ c. Sailing is one of the oldest sports.

3. A sailor must know the language of sailing because he or she
   ☐ a. must understand other sailors.
   ☐ b. must pass an examination.
   ☐ c. won't be allowed to own a sailboat.

4. If a sailboat is not maneuvered carefully inside the breakwater, you can predict that it will
   ☐ a. turn around in circles.
   ☐ b. be hard to slow down.
   ☐ c. hit one of the other boats.

5. Most people who enjoy sailing probably like to be
   ☐ a. scared.
   ☐ b. amused.
   ☐ c. relaxed.

6. Which of the following is a statement of opinion rather than fact?
   ☐ a. Sailing is one of the oldest sports.
   ☐ b. Sailboats are designed in many different styles.
   ☐ c. It is best not to be out on the ocean at or after sunset.

7. When preparing to sail, which is done first?
   ☐ a. The jib is attached to the forestay.
   ☐ b. Battens are put into the sails.
   ☐ c. The dock lines are cast off.

8. Which of the following does *not* fit with the other two?
   ☐ a. dock
   ☐ b. jib
   ☐ c. mainsail

✎ _____ **Number of correct answers** Enter this number on the Critical Thinking graph on page 133.

Vocabulary

Each numbered sentence contains an underlined word from the selection. Following are three definitions. Put an X in the box next to the best meaning of the word as it is used in the sentence.

1. You inhale fresh, clean air.
   ☐ a. choke
   ☐ b. hold back
   ☐ c. breathe in

2. Sailing, when done properly, can be thrilling and <u>exhilarating</u>.
   - ☐ a. tiring
   - ☐ b. exciting
   - ☐ c. defeating

3. Some people want to race, and so need a <u>sleeker</u> design.
   - ☐ a. smoother
   - ☐ b. wider
   - ☐ c. basic

4. There are at least three different "sheets" or lines used to <u>control</u> the sails.
   - ☐ a. manage
   - ☐ b. change
   - ☐ c. put together

5. Setting up <u>requires</u> teamwork.
   - ☐ a. makes
   - ☐ b. pushes
   - ☐ c. needs

6. Careful <u>maneuvering</u> is necessary inside the breakwater where there are usually quite a few other boats.
   - ☐ a. skillful moving
   - ☐ b. active racing
   - ☐ c. gentle swaying

7. Because the wind is a variable, careful planning is needed to allow enough time to reach your <u>destination</u> before dark.
   - ☐ a. person who owns the boat
   - ☐ b. top speed
   - ☐ c. place where you are going

8. Coming in an hour or so before <u>dusk</u> also gives you time to dock the boat.
   - ☐ a. midnight
   - ☐ b. just before dark
   - ☐ c. sunrise

✎ _____ **Number of correct answers**
Enter this number on the Vocabulary graph on page 134.

Personal Response

The author says that coming in an hour or so before dusk gives you time to leave the boat "shipshape" before leaving for home. What do you think *shipshape* means?

_____

_____

_____

✎ **Check Your Progress**
Study the graphs you completed for Lessons 21–30 and answer the How Am I Doing? questions on page 137.

Assessment

Words per Minute

Reading Time	Words per Minute	Reading Time	Words per Minute
1:00	500	4:40	107
1:10	431	4:50	104
1:20	376	5:00	100
1:30	333	5:10	97
1:40	301	5:20	94
1:50	273	5:30	91
2:00	250	5:40	88
2:10	231	5:50	86
2:20	215	6:00	83
2:30	200	6:10	81
2:40	188	6:20	79
2:50	177	6:30	77
3:00	167	6:40	75
3:10	158	6:50	73
3:20	150	7:00	71
3:30	143	7:10	70
3:40	137	7:20	68
3:50	131	7:30	67
4:00	125	7:40	65
4:10	120	7:50	64
4:20	115	8:00	63
4:30	111		

Reading Speed

Directions. Use the graph below to show your reading speed improvement.

First, along the top of the graph, find the lesson number of the selection you just read. Then put a small X on the line directly below the number of the lesson and across from the number of words per minute you read.

As you mark your speed for each lesson, graph your progress by drawing a line to connect the X's. This will help you see right away if your reading speed is going up as it should be. If the line connecting the X's is not going up, see your teacher for advice.

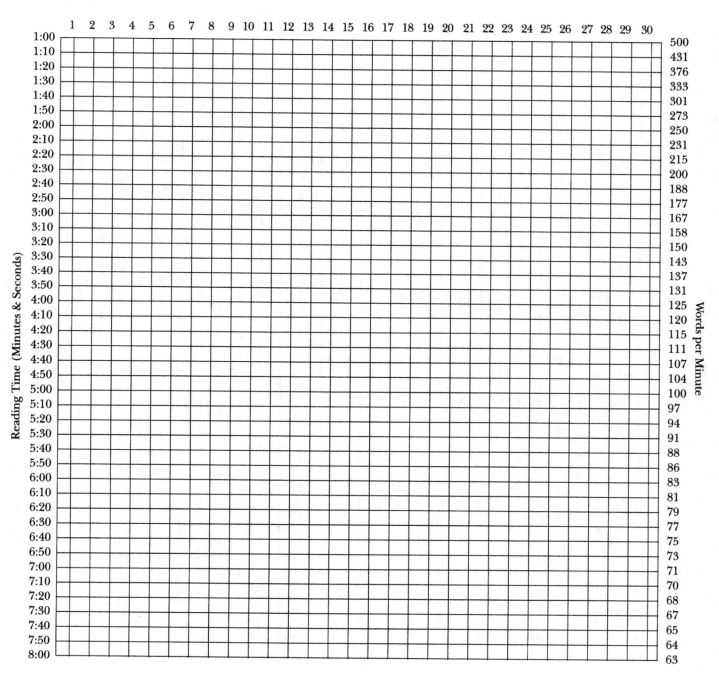

Comprehension

Directions. Use the graph below to show your comprehension scores.

First, along the top of the graph, find the lesson number of the selection you just read. Then put a small X on the line directly below the number of the lesson and across from the score you earned.

As you mark your score for each lesson, graph your progress by drawing a line to connect the X's. This will help you see right away if your comprehension scores are going up or down. If your scores are below 75%, or if they are going down, see your teacher. Try to keep your scores at 75% or above while you continue to build your reading speed.

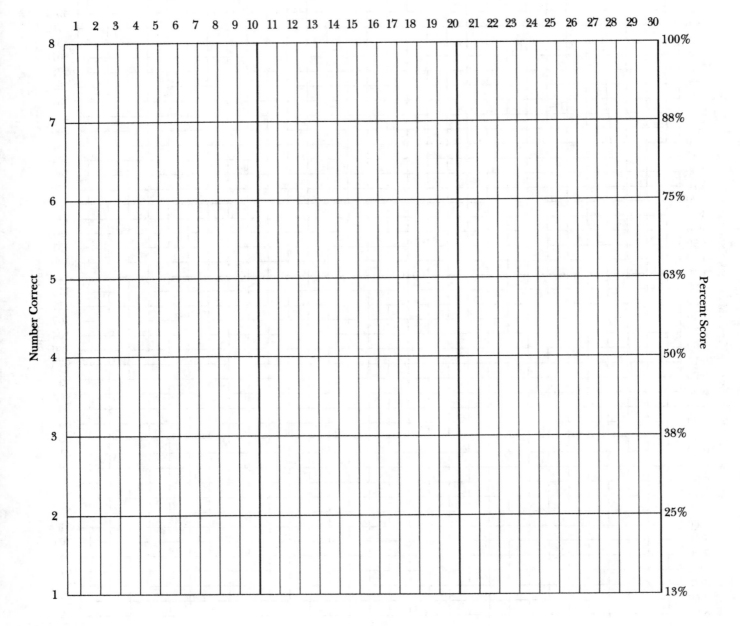

Critical Thinking

Directions. Use the graph below to show your critical thinking scores.

First, along the top of the graph, find the lesson number of the selection you just read. Then put a small X on the line directly below the number of the lesson and across from the score you earned.

As you mark your score for each lesson, graph your progress by drawing a line to connect the X's. This will help you see right away if your critical thinking scores are going up or down. If your scores are below 75%, or if they are going down, see your teacher. Try to keep your scores at 75% or above as you continue to build your reading speed.

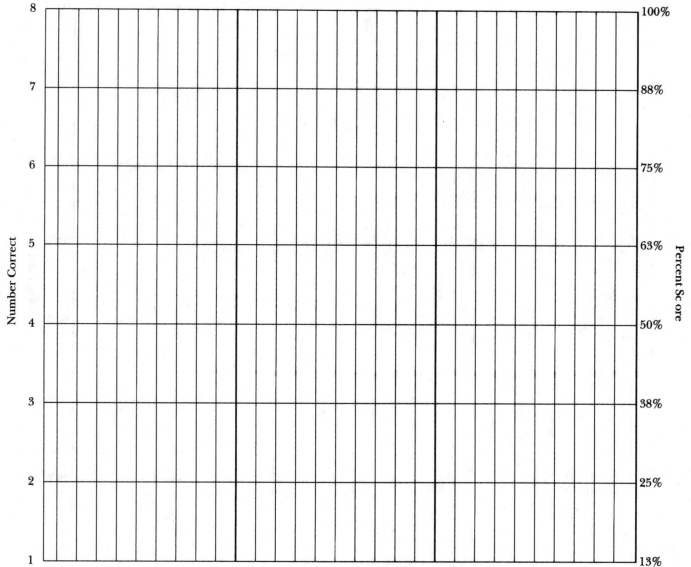

Vocabulary

Directions. Use the graph below to show your vocabulary scores.

First, along the top of the graph, find the lesson number of the selection you just read. Then put a small X on the line directly below the number of the lesson and across from the score you earned.

As you mark your score for each lesson, graph your progress by drawing a line to connect the X's. This will help you see right away if your vocabulary scores are going up or down. If your scores are not going up, see your teacher for advice. Vocabulary scores of 75% are good, but try to earn scores of 88% and 100% when you can.

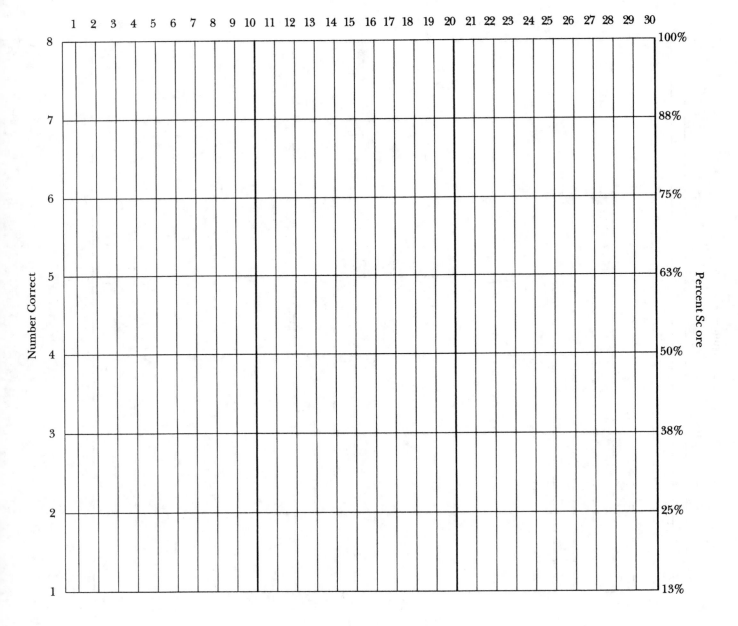

How Am I Doing?

Lessons 1—10

Look back at your completed graphs for lessons 1–10, then answer these questions about your progress.

1. Which lesson are you most proud of? Why?

_____

_____

_____

2. Which lesson did you find most difficult? Why was it difficult?

_____

_____

_____

3. Which type of exercises did you do best: Comprehension, Critical Thinking, or Vocabulary? Why do you think this is true?

_____

_____

_____

4. Which exercises were the most difficult for you? What can you do to correct that?

_____

_____

_____

5. What can you do to improve your reading speed in the following lessons?

_____

_____

_____

How Am I Doing?

Lessons 11—20

Look back at your completed graphs for lessons 11–20, then answer these questions about your progress.

1. How does your reading speed for nonfiction selections compare with your reading speed for fiction selections? Explain.

   _____

   _____

   _____

2. When you read faster do your comprehension scores go up or down? What do you think may be happening?

   _____

   _____

   _____

3. What lesson was most confusing for you? Why?

   _____

   _____

   _____

4. Which type of exercises are still difficult for you—Comprehension, Critical Thinking, or Vocabulary? Why?

   _____

   _____

   _____

5. How can you improve your scores for lessons 21–30? Be specific.

   _____

   _____

   _____

How Am I Doing?

Lessons 21—30

Look back at your completed graphs for lessons 21–30, then answer these questions about your progress.

1. Did your reading speed increase as you completed the lessons in this book? Explain why you think it did or did not.

   _____

   _____

   _____

2. Overall, what was most difficult about the lessons in this book? What was easiest? Explain both answers.

   _____

   _____

   _____

   _____

3. Looking back at your completed progress graphs, where do you see the most improvement? Where do you see the least improvement?

   _____

   _____

   _____

   _____

4. How has completing these lessons affected your everyday reading? Do you read more books for pleasure? Have you been able to read faster and understand concepts better in your textbooks? Are you enjoying reading more? Be specific.

   _____

   _____

   _____